Irene Ivison was a [...] until her 17 year old [...] December 1993. Determined to survive this personal tragedy Irene realised that she had to turn her anger at the dreadful exploitation of her daughter by a pimp into positive action. She is a founder member of the campaigning group CROP (Campaign for the removal of pimps). This group aims to raise public awareness on the issues surrounding coercion of juveniles into prostitution. Irene is also a founder member of Victims Voice, a group working to represent the interest of victims of serious crime and has also played an active role in the development of the self help group, SAMM (Support after Murder/Manslaughter). She lives with her family in Sheffield.

Fiona's Story

Irene Ivison

Some names and place names
have been changed.

A *Virago* Book

Published by Virago Press 1997
Reprinted 1999

A CIP catalogue record for this book is available
from the British Library

ISBN 1 86049 199 5

Typeset by M Rules in Times New Roman
Printed and bound in Great Britain by
Clays Ltd, St Ives plc

Virago
A Division of
Little, Brown and Company (UK)
Brettenham House
Lancaster Place
London WC2E 7EN

This book is dedicated to the memory of our daughter and sister Fiona and also to the memory of all those young girls who were coerced into prostitution and who paid with their lives. Remembering especially Dawn Shields, Maureen Stepan and Natalie Pearman.

Acknowledgements

I wish to thank my children Rebecca and John and all my family and friends whose love and support for me has never wavered.

Other thanks are due to those who helped me to start to regain my life; South Yorkshire Police who dealt with the murder inquiry, in particular Graham Griggs and John Hope, my early mentor John Hattersley, Matthew Mark, Beryl Rayner from CRUSE, Compassionate Friends and SAMM.

I wish to acknowledge the encouragement of Fiona Broadfoot and all my friends and fellow campaigners in CROP. Thanks also to Diana Lamplugh OBE whose example in seeking to make some good come out of evil is a continuing inspiration.

Thanks to Hope Ritchie, Viv Thom and Rony Robinson, my first readers, and to my friends in the Sheffield Hallam Writers Group. Lastly thanks to Tony Whittome for his faith in the book and to Lennie Goodings and Sarah White from Virago who guided me so patiently and kindly through my introduction to the world of book publication.

Foreword

No one reading *Fiona's Story* could remain unaffected by this absorbing and distressing account of the exploitation of young people and youth prostitution. Irene Ivison's simple retelling of her daughter's life has an inevitable fatality about it: how a girl of fourteen, who moves into the urban underworld of drugs, prostitution and violence while remaining essentially an innocent, suffers victimisation, physical abuse and eventually a brutal death. This is a universal tale, and one that has been repeated in a number of British cities. But if there is a meaning to this story, surely it is that Fiona's murder on 17 December 1993 is not something that should just be accepted, or relegated to the status of a tale of one of life's unfortunate victims.

Liberty (the National Council for Civil Liberties), the organisation of which I am Legal Director, became involved with Fiona's story when Irene Ivison contacted our Legal Department and requested advice. From this we were able to identify a wider concern that there should be an open and frank discussion about child prostitution in the United Kingdom. Irene originally asked us if any of the relevant agencies (such as the police and social services) from whom she had sought help and who had, in her view, failed adequately to protect Fiona, could be held responsible in negligence. In the end, we had no choice but to advise her that, as a matter of public policy, whether any of the agencies had been negligent or not, she would not be able even to attempt to sue any of those bodies.

This book is a testament to the fact that the matter cannot rest there. Although Irene may have no remedy in law, Fiona's story demands answers not only because the law has failed her mother, but also because, arguably, the relevant agencies may not have recognised that Fiona was at risk. It is for this reason that we are supporting Irene in her request that Sheffield City Council hold a Public Inquiry into the events that led to Fiona's death. That Inquiry should not just examine how Fiona died, but also what led her into prostitution and what the law enforcement agencies could, or should, have done to prevent this.

But this demand for an Inquiry is not about seeking to point fingers of blame in individual cases. It is now a bigger issue. A debate on child prostitution and exploitation in the United Kingdom, and its causes, consequences and extent is of pressing urgency. At the time of writing, there is considerable political and media interest in the appropriate treatment of child sexual abusers. Arguments for and against registration of such people have tended to dwell on the stereotypical image of the child abuser. Yet, as *Fiona's Story* shows, there are many ways in which children become vulnerable to exploitation. Protecting young people, such as Fiona, from being intimidated into prostitution should be a priority.

From Irene's account, we learn that throughout Fiona's life, she had a trusting and loving relationship with her mother. From Fiona's first encounter with Zebbi, Irene sensed that her daughter was at risk and so sought police protection. Fiona was fourteen at the time. Zebbi introduced her to Sheffield street culture, and it was not long before Fiona began a relationship with another man, Elroy. It was at this time that she stopped going to school. She told her mother that she was taking drugs and having under-age sex with Elroy.

It is of little consolation now that the judge who sentenced Fiona's murderer, Allan Duffy, to life recognised the role her mother played in trying to protect her. It is reported that he said:

> I sympathise with Mrs Ivison. She did all any mother could possibly have done. It was a dreadful situation, she has everyone's sympathy.[1]

No one disputes that it is difficult for a parent to protect a teenager who wants to 'live her own life'. The police and social services could do nothing without Fiona's consent, but for her mother there are profound and unanswered questions about whether these agencies might have done more. Fiona was recognised as a young person in law and as such an extra duty was owed to her.[2]

Irene first approached Liberty's Legal Department at the end of October 1996. She could not accept that her daughter's death was simply a tragic and unique event. From the research carried out while writing this book, she had identified that the circumstances that led to Fiona's murder were by no means uncommon. On the contrary, through her conversations with other parents in her position, she had come to realise that the seduction of girls and young women into prostitution follows a similar pattern time and time again. She met many other mothers and fathers who, like her, felt helpless and let down by the police, social services and local education authorities. Irene asked whether there was anyway she could legally challenge the way the police and/or social services had responded to Fiona's situation.

I explained to her that her chances of success were slim. In another case involving the parent of a murder victim who sought to sue the police in negligence for failure to protect their daughter from Peter Sutcliffe, the Yorkshire Ripper, the House of Lords held that as a general principle the police are immune from actions in negligence as a matter of public policy.[3] However, Fiona's circumstances were not parallel to the victims in the Ripper case. She was not one of a vast number of the female

---

[1] *Sheffield Journal*, 16 February 1995.
[2] The Children Act 1989, Section 17(1) provides a general duty upon the local authority to ensure the welfare of children.
[3] *Hill v. Chief Constable of the West Yorkshire Police* [1989] 1 AC 53.

public at risk. Given the situation into which she had been led, there was a high probability that Fiona would come to harm, and it would not have been incredible to have assumed that this could include her murder. I was equally unsure that no cause of action lay against the social services.[4] At the very least, it seemed to me that they could have informed Irene that she might issue an injunction against Elroy, preventing him from going anywhere near Fiona.

I applied for legal aid for Irene. Legal aid was refused. However, at this stage we were approaching the time limit for starting an action. Irene had to issue a writ within three years of Fiona's death. We appealed against the Legal Aid Board decision and had no choice, in order to preserve our position, but to issue a writ against South Yorkshire Police and Sheffield City Council before that appeal could be heard. In January 1997 Irene's appeal was heard. Despite the fact that the public policy immunity laid down in the Ripper case can have exceptions and has been successfully challenged before the European Commission of Human Rights,[5] the Legal Aid Board turned down the appeal.

Paradoxically, that hearing turned out to be Irene's only opportunity to state her case before a tribunal. She was challenged on the grounds that she could not establish causation, a legal term meaning that, but for the police and social service's alleged negligence, Fiona would not have been murdered.

Under the circumstances, Irene responded magnificently. Brushing me aside, she told the tribunal that a clear link had been established between the exploitation and seduction into prostitution of young girls, all of whom are in their early teens when they are taken up by their future pimps, and the violence they inevitably suffer as a consequence. As she has since pointed out to me, had Fiona been engaging in unlawful sexual relations

---

[4] Although there is a similar public policy immunity from claiming damages from a breach of duty owed by the social services. (*X (minors) v. Bedfordshire CC* [1995] 3 All ER)

[5] *Osman v UK*, Application No. 23452/94

with an uncle or cousin, she would not be subjected to such a test of causation.

Irene had no legal aid and no counsel's opinion advising her whether or not she should proceed. She made it clear that if she had the resources, she would pay for such legal advice. In the event, two barristers generously agreed to advise Irene. They wrote her an opinion and we had a three-hour conference where they explained to Irene why she could not succeed in suing either the police or Sheffield City Council.

This story highlights the problems surrounding the public policy immunity from suing the police and social services for their perceived failure to act. This book leaves the reader with the sense that more might have been done to protect Fiona. However, the law as it stands is unable to offer a remedy. Regardless of the facts, and whether or not anyone was at fault, Irene cannot sue because the House of Lords has said that she cannot sue. The immunity remains intact.

Because Allan Duffy pleaded guilty to Fiona's murder there was no trial and the evidence of how she came to be a prostitute and be murdered was never put to the court. Additionally, due to its limited scope, all that Fiona's inquest could establish was how she died. Consequently, Irene has been denied the opportunity to review the circumstances that led to Fiona's death. As this book makes plain, Irene has many questions, which, at the present time, have been unanswered.

This is a further reason why Liberty is supporting Irene's request for a Public Inquiry into all the circumstances that led to Fiona's murder. That Inquiry should be empowered to make recommendations and issue guidelines. It appears that there were problems in the monitoring and management of Fiona's case, and even if no one is to blame or can be held responsible, it should be incumbent upon the police and social services to seek to ensure that, to the best of everyone's abilities, they never occur again.

Fiona's Story makes very distressing reading. The impact on the Ivison family of the situation leading to Fiona's death is retold in an alarmingly honest and candid way. I admire Irene for her best efforts to try to keep her family together, not only during Fiona's lifetime but in the wake of her murder and during her struggle to receive some official recognition that her daughter's death could possibly have been avoided.

Fiona comes across as a feisty though innocent girl. Her passion and commitment to fighting social injustice reminds me of many of the volunteers at Liberty. Such people keep the organisation going and maintain our resolve. Irene's description of her own and Fiona's naivety at times make the reader smile. And, they are not the only compassionate figures. One of the most memorable aspects of the book is the sensitive way in which the police helped Irene come to terms with Fiona's death. The individual officers involved were totally selfless and clearly played a vital role in helping Irene in those first few weeks.

Irene's frank and moving narrative of the struggles in her daughter's life is filled with humanity and loving detail. It is also a story of our time and deals with a number of issues which confront us all, both individually and as a society. It demonstrates the need for reform. Reform not only of police and social services procedures for prioritisation, but also of a more fundamental nature, ensuring that those agencies are adequately resourced.

A Public Inquiry of the type proposed would be in a position to make recommendations on such issues. It should be chaired by an eminent and respected individual, and should focus on how the schools, the police and the social services could work together with teenagers and their families to ensure that they receive appropriate protection. In an atmosphere of trust and understanding not only on the part of the families but also the responsible agencies, situations such as Fiona's, where a vulnerable young girl was forced to work the streets with its tragic result, might in future be avoided.

Jonathan Cooper, Legal Director at Liberty,
London, February 1997

Prologue

'The body of a young woman, aged between 15 and 22 years, has been found in a multi-storey car park in Doncaster . . .' As I read the words in the newspaper, I froze in horror, I knew instantly that it was my daughter Fiona whose battered and strangled body had been found, early on that cold December morning.

When I thought about it afterwards, I realised that it was the first time I hadn't been worried sick when Fiona had not returned home as expected. Maybe this was because there was no longer any point in my anxiety for her. She had at last been freed from her troubled existence and was no longer around on this earth. Her own prediction of her early death had been fulfilled and she was finally at peace.

I had last seen Fiona alive on Friday evening, 17 December. She told me she was going out clubbing in Doncaster, with a man she had been associating with. He was known as 'Zebbi', his Rastafarian name. She didn't return home on Saturday morning, but Zebbi rang for her. He told me that he had dropped Fiona back in Sheffield, late the previous night. He said she had told him she was going to visit some friends. I found out later that this was a lie: Fiona had never left Doncaster. She lay all night in the car park until her body was found in the morning.

When she had still not returned home on Sunday, I reported her missing to the police. It was only after I had done this that I picked up the paper and read the article. Straight away, I knew it was Fiona. Fear gripped me and I went weak. I sank to my knees and prayed desperately that it wasn't her, but I knew, oh God, I knew that it was, and so I begged to be given the strength to endure what was to follow.

The phone rang and I grabbed it. It was the Sheffield Police. 'Is your daughter home?'

'No,' I screamed, 'but I've just read about the body in Doncaster. Has it been identified yet?'

The voice on the other end of the phone tried to calm me: 'We're checking on everything. Don't panic.'

I paced up and down the room. John and Rebecca, my other two children, were already in bed and I was on my own. I fought the rising panic and struggled to remain calm, but it was impossible. My stomach was knotted in fear. The phone rang again. This time it was the Doncaster Police. Two officers from the serious crime squad were on their way to speak to me. Now I knew without doubt that the nightmare was real.

When the two men arrived they were very kind. They already knew, from my description of Fiona on the missing person report, that they would have to confirm my terrible fear. My daughter Fiona, seventeen years old, had been murdered. We would never see her alive again, never see her pretty face light up with laughter, never, ever again be shocked by her exploits and adventures.

I was numb with shock that night. A young policewoman arrived to sit with me. We didn't sleep. In the morning, worse was to follow. I learned that Fiona had been working as a street prostitute in Doncaster for the previous two weeks. I had had no idea, but she had told her young sister, Rebecca. Apparently Zebbi had been taking her to Doncaster's red light area. He had been overheard threatening her with a 'battering' if she didn't get money for him. Fiona had also told another young friend that she was frightened of him, and so, stoked up with drugs, she had stood on the street and sold her body.

Words cannot describe how I felt at this revelation. I couldn't believe that Fiona had become a prostitute, but thinking back now over her life, it seems to me that the path she trod was only too likely to lead her to this very violent and tragic end.

A week after the murder, the killer was found: Allan Duffy, a white man of twenty-six, who killed her when she became frightened of him. Fourteen months later he pleaded guilty to her murder and is now serving life imprisonment.

The pimp, Zebbi, insisting upon his right to silence, turned his face to the wall and refused to co-operate with the police. He remains at liberty.

Nothing in my early life could have prepared me for the tragedy which was to shatter the happiness of my family. As far as I can see there were no indications or pointers giving any clue as to what was to happen.

I was born and reared in the university town of Oxford. My childhood was happy and secure. My parents were Irish. They had come to England in the early 1940s and my father had found work at the Cowley Ironworks. Our family settled happily in Oxford. Every other year we would return to see our relatives in Dublin for our holidays. I still retain an abiding love for Eire and her people and look back with nostalgia on those days.

My early school years were spent at the nearest Roman Catholic school. I was a bright enough child and passed the eleven plus examination, gaining my passport to a grammar school education. I became a pupil at a small convent school run by the Sisters of Notre Dame. My years there were tranquil and happy.

After taking A levels, I decided on a career as a physiotherapist. At eighteen I moved away from my family, spending three years as a student physiotherapist at the

Bristol Royal Infirmary. I was given a grant by the Ministry of Health for my training, with the condition that I work for a minimum of one year in an NHS hospital after qualification. I moved to Sheffield, where I had some friends, intending to do the required year and then look for a job abroad.

How different I found Sheffield from the south of England! I was struck by the grime and squalor of this sprawling, once great city. Industry had left its mark upon Sheffield with its blackened walls and houses. I loved the countryside surrounding the city, its stark bleak moors a stunning contrast to the rolling green hills of the Mendips around Bristol and the lush green valleys and plains of Oxfordshire.

My plans to spend a minimum of time here and then to work abroad were completely abandoned when I met the man who was to become my husband and the father of my three children. I fell in love with him immediately and shortly after our meeting he had asked me to marry him. We married in 1970 and bought our first house in Chapeltown, a Sheffield suburb. At this time I started to work with disabled children, an area of work which I stayed in for the next twenty-three years.

We delayed having a family until 1975 when, to my delight, I found I was pregnant. Fiona was born on 5 February 1976, a much loved and cherished child. I cry now when I remember my baby; I can't bear to think

5

about what happened to her. I loved her with every ounce of my being, as only a mother can love her child.

Did you ever love a child, Duffy? Seventeen years later you murdered this precious infant of mine. Did you never love a child like that? You can't have done or you would never have harmed her. Can you conceive of the suffering you caused me when you unleashed your anger and frustration on my beautiful girl? I loved her then and for every minute of her seventeen years, no matter what she did. She was Fiona, a special child, I had held her close, nurtured and cared for her, and you smashed her in your blind, unthinking, murderous rage. I will never understand what you did to Fiona and my family. There are no answers. I only know that when I held Fiona at her birth, I loved her so much that I would have died rather than see her hurt – my precious, beautiful, wonderful child.

Fiona's Story

In 1975 we had moved from our house in Chapeltown to an older semi with a large garden in Totley, a fairly affluent suburb on the south-west side of the city. This is where Fiona was conceived. I had loved the place when I first saw it, mainly because of its private, secluded position, set back from the road up a small private lane. However, it was not to be a happy house for me. I learned later that, a few years previously, the son of the then householder had committed suicide in one of the downstairs rooms. When I am musing, I often wonder whether his unhappy spirit was reincarnated into Fiona, causing her to have a very troubled young life.

We had delayed starting a family for longer than I would have wished. My husband had started to have grave doubts as to the advisability of bringing children into the world. He was quite right to think seriously about this issue. Too many people embark on parenthood without giving much thought to what is involved.

But my biological clock was ticking away and I found it hard to imagine a future without children.

This matter was to cause some conflict between us, eventually resolved when my husband decided that it was unfair of him to deny my maternal longings. So the decision was taken to start our family. I was always very aware that the choice to have children was largely mine, and it was for this reason that I felt myself to be largely responsible for their upbringing. Years later, when we had divorced and I was trying to manage Fiona's difficulties, I probably didn't ask her father for enough help precisely because I was still sensitive to the fact that he would have chosen to remain childless; I thought it would be unfair to burden him with the problems which one of our children was causing.

During my first pregnancy I felt none of these forebodings. I was one of those fortunate women who actually bloom. I was in awe of the whole process and read avidly every book on childbirth I could lay my hands on. I marvelled at the growing foetus in each stage of its development. I couldn't wait for the pregnancy to show and in the early months I would stuff a pillow up my jumper and strut in front of the mirror, trying to imagine what it would be like as my body swelled with the growing child. I was, however, thoroughly frightened at the thought of actually giving birth and secretly hoped that I might need a Caesarean section. I had read too many horrifying tales of women

8

suffering agonies in childbirth, writhing and gripping the bedrails with whitened knuckles. I found it hard to believe that the relaxation and breathing exercises taught in the ante-natal classes would be of any use whatsoever.

As the delivery date approached, my mother-in-law came down from her home in Carlisle to stay with us. I always enjoyed her company and we happily talked away the waiting hours. Fiona chose not to arrive on the predicted date and when she still had not put in an appearance two weeks later, I was admitted to the maternity unit for the birth to be induced. With hindsight, I wish I had had the courage to refuse the induction and let the birth proceed as nature had intended. Poor Fiona, yanked unceremoniously into the world before she was ready, and violently dispatched out of it when she was only seventeen.

I was admitted to the hospital on the evening of 4 February. I was so excited I was unable to eat more than a bowl of home-made soup all day. The induction was supposed to be started off early the following morning. In the event a lot of babies must have chosen to put in an appearance that day because I was not taken up to the theatre until 6 p.m. I remember feeling quite weak from lack of food, hardly a fit state for the hard work that was to follow.

Fiona's birth was a chaotic nightmare, at times verging on the farcical. I was wired up to a foetal monitoring machine which, via an electrode attached to the baby's head, was supposed to warn of imminent foetal distress. I could see the monitor quite clearly and was very alarmed when the dancing line indicating the baby's heartbeat suddenly changed to a straight line.

'My God,' I cried, 'my baby has died.'

It was quickly established, however, that there was a fault in the machine and not the baby. My husband (actually a medical physics technician) rectified the fault and we carried on. This happened again at least twice, by which time no one was taking any notice of it at all.

Labour proceeded very rapidly, I was given pethidine and then gas and air as I started to experience the 'pushing' contractions which should have expelled my baby out into the world. But no matter how hard I pushed and pushed, nothing happened. By this time I was frantic, sending myself silly on gas and air and begging for an epidural. It seemed the anaesthetist was nowhere to be found. By the time he eventually turned up with a team of doctors, I wasn't too sure where I was at all. I can recall a man with extremely hairy arms standing at the foot of the bed with some forceps. Thankfully the epidural was administered, the forceps applied to turn Fiona into the correct position for her journey down the birth canal and she at last emerged into the world.

I was so out of it that I remember feeling faintly surprised at suddenly seeing a baby on my chest and hearing 'Hairy Arms' saying, 'What a perfectly beautiful baby.'

Fiona was a beautiful baby. She weighed 7 lb 6 oz. She wasn't at all red and wrinkled, like some babies are at birth. She gave her first cry and then slept peacefully. I was taken back up, with my baby and husband, to the post-natal ward. By now it was about 10 p.m. I was feeling a little cheated as the birth had not been at all like I had expected. I thought I might at least be given a cup of tea now, as in all the books I had read the proud mother always enjoys a cup of tea. I was determined not to be done out of this part of the process. A cup of tea was brought from somewhere and I was promptly sick. At this point I gave up and sank into an exhausted sleep, content that Fiona was sleeping beside me in her cot.

At intervals during the night I woke up and looked at my baby with wonder. She was so beautiful and, in my eyes, she was perfect. I lay there gazing at her, stroking her tiny face with my finger, entranced.

It was during one of these moments that I became aware that my bed was soaked in blood. I immediately rang for a nurse and told her about it. She said they were very busy and without even looking in the bed gave me some paracetamol and bustled off. I was still too doped to kick up a fuss and drifted off to sleep. In the morning when I awoke properly and tried to sit up I kept fainting. I had obviously been haemorrhaging in the night and had lost a lot of blood. The nurses were horrified when they looked in my bed and discovered the situation.

Things went from bad to worse during my stay. I was dreadfully sore from the episiotomy and by the seventh day could barely walk. I was bent double.

'Do you always walk like that?' one young nurse asked me. 'Have you got something wrong with you?'

I was so green. This was my first baby. I didn't know what to expect. I had never had stitches before and I had assumed that my pain was a normal consequence of a difficult birth.

One evening the nurse taking my temperature discovered it was very high. She shook the thermometer down, stuck it in my mouth again for about one second, and then said, 'Oh, it's OK now. I must have read it wrong the first time.'

That night I had a ferocious nightmare. Wild horses were galloping towards me. I could hear their thundering hooves pounding loudly in my brain – over and over. They knocked fear into the very pit of my stomach until I awoke in a sweat of terror. I felt really ill. That morning I was due to go home. I couldn't wait to get out of the hospital even though I was far from fit.

I arrived home with Fiona, happy to have my mum-in-law there to care for us. My own mother, who still lived in Oxford, was unable to help as my father was not well enough to travel and she couldn't leave him. I slept fitfully that first night in between getting up at regular intervals to feed Fiona. In the morning I awoke to find the bed absolutely drenched in a foul liquid. For the first time I had no pain as I moved. It suddenly clicked with me what the problem had been: I had had an enormous stitch abscess, hence the fever, the nightmares and my painful walk. It had burst in the night and of course I immediately felt better. The abscess had been undetected by the nursing staff.

It was not a good start. I was really unwell for quite a while. I did complain about my treatment in the hospital and was invited to discuss with the matron what had gone wrong. It appeared that they were very busy during the time I spent there. I wasn't even down on the cardex as being a patient until three days after my admission. Apparently the nurse in charge of the ward on the night I was admitted was not well herself. The matron was very apologetic and assured me that they would tighten up their standards. I accepted the apology but was to feel cheated for a long time that what should have been a memorable, happy experience had turned so sour.

Fiona was an absolutely dreadful baby. What on earth ailed her I don't know. From the start she demanded constant attention, content only when firmly attached to my breast as she suckled. I was determined to breastfeed. At the time the trend was turning away from bottlefeeding. People were beginning to realise that nature's way of nurturing babies was a good idea and midwives were actively encouraging mothers to breastfeed. Unfortunately the emphasis was still on rigid timing. In hospital I was given a chart and told that I was only to feed Fiona at four-hourly intervals. If I fed her on demand I would be 'making a rod for my own back', and she would become quite spoilt. I quickly discovered that there was no way Fiona was going to accept this schedule and fed her on demand, guiltily making up the times on the chart so it looked as if I was doing as I'd been told. I didn't know enough about babies then to realise that I was, of course, right, and I can remember feeling quite confused and guilty about my deception.

I was soon exhausted. Fiona never went willingly into her cot to sleep. Worse still, she used to wake at two-hourly intervals in the night and only the comfort of me feeding her would settle her down. In desperation I bought a dummy but she spat this out in great disgust. She refused juice from a bottle with the same contempt. This went on for eight months. I was like a zombie. I have always needed a lot of sleep; I didn't know what had hit me.

Right from the start Fiona was very clingy and would never go to other people, even close family. In those early days she was always crying. I can remember my neighbour suggesting on one occasion that there might be something wrong with her. On her advice, I took Fiona to the doctor. To my surprise, she actually had an ear infection. Because she cried so much all the time, there was no difference when she was ill, no reason to suspect that anything was wrong. I have great sympathy now with anyone whose first baby is like this – and there are plenty. I had not imagined caring for a baby would be so difficult. My confidence was shattered. What was I doing wrong?

Eventually, however, as Fiona grew, the situation improved. She discovered her cot blanket had a fringe of tassels which she would twiddle as she went off to sleep. This blanket came to be known as 'Fringe'. She also became very attached to a woolly doll, a 'bovver boy' called Robert which her Nana in Leeds had knitted for her. Robert and Fringe went everywhere with her. They now lie entombed with her in her last resting place, counting the midnight stars in the cemetery on Abbey Lane.

Fiona was one of those babies who develop very quickly. I can remember the first word she spoke, when she was only eight months old. We were looking at a Ladybird picture book and she quite clearly said 'apple' when we came to a picture of one. I was so proud of my bright baby. She was walking by the time she was a year old and you could have an interesting conversation with her by eighteen months. I used to read to her for hours on end. She loved books and would toddle up with one demanding to be read to whenever I sat down.

First signs of her immersing herself into fantasy showed very early. Once when we were out shopping an elderly lady stopped to talk with her in her pushchair.

'What's your name?' she asked, to which Fiona replied, 'Ali Baba.'

Highly amused, the lady asked me for Fiona's real name which I told her, while Fiona protested indignantly, 'I'm not Fiona. I'm Ali Baba.'

My father had died when Fiona was four months old and my mother had come to live near us in Sheffield. I was very pleased with her decision. She and Fiona were great pals. Mum spent hours playing with her. One day a visit to Granny's flat resulted in disaster: Fiona fell and knocked all of her front teeth out. Her screams and the blood were appalling. We rushed to the Children's Hospital casualty unit and from there to the nearby Dental Hospital. This incident was to leave its mark on Fiona and she never afterwards attended either doctor or dentist without kicking up the most dreadful fuss. Unfortunately, the accident meant she had to have quite extensive dental treatment. My dentist was always extremely patient with her. At one point, he used to examine Fiona's teeth with both of us lying in the dentist's chair, Fiona spreadeagled on top of me, no mean feat when she was eleven.

I used to spend a lot of time out walking with Fiona in her pushchair. Looking back now, I know I was extremely anxious for her. Maybe all new mothers experience feelings of foreboding and doom at times for their children, but in those early days there were moments when I was almost overwhelmed. I didn't have the same experience with either Rebecca or John, my younger children; it was only for Fiona that I was afraid. Once, when she was quite small, we'd walked right up to the top of a hill near our house and I suddenly had a powerful urge to leap with her down the hill into oblivion. I can distinctly remember thinking that maybe it would be better for both of us. I wasn't seriously contemplating suicide, but sometimes thoughts like these would invade my mind unexpectedly. I may have been suffering from post-natal depression or still debilitated from the birth. They were, nevertheless, very disturbing experiences.

As Fiona progressed through infancy, we did the usual rounds of Mother and Toddler clubs and coffee mornings with other mums and their offspring. Fiona would behave appallingly and these occasions became an ordeal for me. Why I persisted, I really don't know. I suppose I had come to accept the view that all children must have company and learn how to socialise from a very early age, regardless of their own temperament. The truth is that she was quite self-contained. She was a perfectionist, even at two years old. If another toddler came and knocked down her tower of bricks or inadvertently spoiled her sand castle, she would turn puce with rage. She could amuse herself for hours on end and, at that age, really didn't want the company of other toddlers, especially not annoying ones who ruined her pleasures.

I had not intended to return to work, having resigned from my job when Fiona was born, but when she was eighteen months, I was offered two mornings' work as a physio at a local hospice for terminally ill patients. It seemed ideal, as there was a crèche where Fiona could stay while I worked. We thought it was worth a try and the extra money would come in handy. Fiona decided otherwise. She just would not settle in the nursery at all and screamed frantically every time I left her. I was completely unable to reassure her. I realised how badly she was affected when, every time we put our coats on, even when we were only going to the shops, she would cry, 'Not going to nursery, Mummy!' After four weeks I gave in and resigned. I didn't attempt another return to work until Fiona was old enough to go to school.

In the meantime I decided to take the opportunity of continuing my education. I enrolled on an Open University degree course, studying a social science foundation course and eventually completing my degree in economics. This degree must be one of the most hard-earned ones in the Open University. It spanned eight years, three children, part-time employment and a divorce. I did one exam in a very late stage of pregnancy when I could barely get behind the desk. On another occasion, I breastfed my son John in an economics lecture full of men. To their credit, nobody turned a hair.

I often feel now that, as a woman, I had a poor deal.

I was conned. I had been socialised into thinking that I should be a superwoman – able to cope efficiently with house, husband and children, yet maintaining my intelligence and always looking attractive, not letting myself go. Well, I definitely wasn't a superwoman. Basically, I was an exhausted wreck. I was always tired. With hindsight, and the feminist in me finds it hard to admit this, I would have been better devoting myself entirely to my young family. Then, I believed it would turn me into a boring cabbage. I thought that the mundane tasks associated with rearing a young family were less worthy than a bright academic career. I do not feel this way now.

Three years after Fiona, I had my second daughter, Rebecca. Again I had been really well during the pregnancy and looked forward to welcoming a second child into our family. Rebecca was born on 15 March 1979. Her birth was much easier than Fiona's. I woke up at 4 a.m. and realised that labour had started. I roused my husband, alerted my mother, who was staying with us to look after Fiona, and we set off for the hospital.

After a bath and the indignity of the enema, I was put to bed in a small side room down a corridor from the delivery suite. My husband had decided not to witness this birth and returned home to Fiona and Granny. I had been in bed about thirty minutes when the contractions started to get really strong and then, very soon afterwards, I felt the urge to push. I rang the bell to summon a nurse. When she appeared, I told her, between contractions, and in my polite, well-brought-up voice, 'I think I'm about to have this baby.'

Then she actually asked me, 'Do you think you could just hang on for a minute as we're in the middle of a meeting?'

This always amuses me now, as the number of meetings in hospitals seems to have grown out of all proportion – even the smallest action needing a meeting before it can be implemented. At this point another strong contraction took over and the nurse was forced to take me seriously. I was whipped on to a trolley, rushed down to the delivery suite and just made it on to the bed as Rebecca was born, a big beautiful baby, weighing 9 lb, already looking older than new-born. I held her to my breast and she suckled contentedly. I felt marvellous.

The rest of the family came to visit us later that day, Fiona clutching Robert and Fringe and curious to see her new sister. We had bought her a toy cash register and told her it was a present to her from Rebecca. She was delighted by both the toy and her baby sister.

As Rebecca grew older, every year on her birthday she would ask me to tell her the story of her birth and I would relate this tale of her bringing the toy cash register for Fiona. On the eve of Rebecca's fifteenth birthday, Fiona had been dead for three months. Once again, as I sat on Rebecca's bed, she asked me for her birth story.

I'd got as far as her giving the toy before we couldn't go on, Rebecca, tears streaming down her face, cried, 'I don't want any more birthdays without my sister.'

What could I say to her? I could give no comfort. There was none at all for us at that time.

Rebecca was a delight as a baby. She did everything according to the book, sleeping after a feed, and even managing to go through the night without waking up when she was only four months old. She restored my confidence in myself as a mother. I realised that I wasn't to blame for my difficulties with Fiona as a baby (though the circumstances of her birth and my nervousness as a first-time mother can't have helped); it was more that her acutely sensitive nature made her more demanding and she needed more demonstrations of love and security than the average child.

Fiona loved having a baby sister and we all settled down happily together. On one occasion that summer, I left Rebecca sitting outside in her baby chair watching Fiona play in the sandpit their daddy had made for them. Fiona decided that Rebecca needed a hat. When I came out to check them, there was Rebecca, smiling proudly, with a neat dampened sand hat covering her little bald head. It was quite perfect, rather like those caps worn by Jewish boys at their Bar Mitzvah and, to add effect, Fiona had decorated it all around the edge with Smarties. Rebecca was such a good baby. She just sat there, with a wide beam.

'Doesn't it suit her, Mummy?' Fiona exclaimed, and of course I said, 'Yes, it really does.'

On another occasion, Rebecca's second winter, they both went outside to play in the snow, warmly wrapped up in layers of jumpers and snow suits. When I looked out on them a few minutes later, there was Rebecca, soundly asleep, propped up against a snowman, with not a care in the world.

They were so different, these two, Fiona surviving on a bare minimum of sleep, Rebecca dropping off, no matter what the situation, if she was tired.

Fifteen months later my son, John, arrived. His birth, like the other two, was very quick. I went into labour at 6 a.m. We drove to the maternity unit where I was put through the familiar preparatory drill. At eight, the consultant visited me in the small side ward. Barely acknowledging me, he ran through my gynaecological history with his entourage and then said, 'I think we'd better get her going on an oxytocin drip to speed up the labour.'

Remembering the fiasco of Fiona's birth, there was no way I was going to allow any intervention this time, so I ventured to ask him why he felt it was necessary.

'You are what is known as "elderly" as far as child-bearing is concerned,' he told me, 'and we don't like prolonged labours in this hospital.'

'But I've never had a long labour,' I protested, 'and if you don't mind I won't have the drip at the moment. If

I haven't had this baby within the next four hours, I might consider it.'

The entourage looked amazed at this outburst. Nevertheless the consultant let me have my way and, sure enough, two hours later, John made his entrance into the world. I felt a great deal of satisfaction, especially when one of the young doctors came in to see me afterwards and, with a big wink, said, 'You were right, weren't you?'

And of course I was.

Our family was now complete. It was very hard work looking after three children under five. While Rebecca did sleep through the night, John took a long time to settle into a routine and, for Fiona, the day often began at 5 a.m. I was constantly exhausted. It was round about this time that our marriage began to crumble.

Shortly after John was born, I had what I can only describe as a spiritual experience. My husband's father, also John, was diagnosed with terminal cancer. He had been hospitalised but, soon after his prognosis was certain, he was allowed home to Leeds to live out his remaining months with his second wife, Isobel. On the night he came home from hospital, Isobel rang us to let us know that he was home and that they had spent a happy evening watching TV. We retired to bed. I fell into my usual exhausted sleep and had an amazing dream. I saw a door opening behind which was the most beautiful golden light. I knew in my dream that this was a very wonderful, peaceful, loving light and I marvelled at its radiance. The loud shrill of the phone startled us both out of our sleep. My husband ran to answer it. It was Isobel.

'Your dad has just died, very peacefully,' she told him.

I thought afterwards that the timing of my dream was pure coincidence and that my father-in-law's condition must have been playing on my mind as I drifted into sleep. Yet he had not been expected to die so quickly and that light behind the door was unforgettable.

I was to experience it again some fourteen years later after Fiona died – its peaceful, loving radiance – unexplainable in any human terms yet very real – leaving an immense impression upon me.

I have to say that at this time I was floundering in relation to the meaning of God. Established religion had let me down badly and I felt that all of the associated dogma, pomp and ceremony were far removed from the true meaning of our spirituality and indeed often deflected us from it. I now live by and believe in only one creed, which is that of love. As far as I can see, the only answer to humanity's problems today is to love and care for one another in every aspect of our lives.

If 'God is love', then so be it, I am a believer.

One evening when the children were small, I went to the local Methodist Church Hall for a screening of *The War Game*, a documentary film showing the effects an atom bomb would have if launched on a big city. The film had originally been banned by the BBC because of its horrifying content. The next day, watching my children play, I couldn't forget it. I was appalled at the inhumanity of mankind. How had we become capable of making weapons such as these which could wipe out whole populations in an instant? I was also very angry that the lives of my children could be threatened in this way. I hate violence. It is the refuge of the bully who can't reason with his intelligence. It indicates not who is right, merely who is physically stronger.

Over the next few years, after seeing this film, I became active in the local peace movement and CND. I tried hard to bring my children up with a philosophy of non-violence, hoping they would be able to reason with their minds and not their fists, and when this was not possible, to turn the other cheek.

Those early childhood years passed quickly. All three were strong-minded little characters, especially Fiona. She was extremely imaginative, sensitive and stubborn. We had some terrible battles of will. She could scream for hours on end to prove her point.

There were other young children in the neighbouring houses and they would often play together. Sometimes they would play happily, other times there were clashes. On one occasion, which I remember vividly, a neighbour's child was pulling the heads off the dandelions outside our garden. Fiona loved the dandelions and to her this was an act of desecration. She asked him to stop. When he persisted, she screamed at him to go away. When he still wouldn't stop, Fiona couldn't cope with it and told the child that he wasn't allowed on the land outside our gate. It was, of course, quite wrong of her to say this, but I was appalled when he went to his home and reported to his parents what Fiona had said. I was even more amazed when the whole incident almost turned into a territorial dispute.

Fiona was always managing to make herself look at fault. She had no guile. If she was upset or felt that something was unfair, she was incapable of keeping it to herself. Another child wouldn't have been too bothered about the dandelions, but Fiona just could not ignore it. The trouble was that her behaviour was often misinterpreted, and she usually came out of it the loser. Her response to what she considered an unfairness was usually so extreme that the initial cause of the problem would be lost, and Fiona's behaviour would become the issue.

There were a lot of happy times too. Fiona was excellent at devising games. We had a big bright orange blanket-bag full of dressing-up clothes, mainly obtained from jumble sales. Fiona would write plays and the children would perform them for us. She would also immerse herself in fantasy. One whole summer she was Flash Gordon. She insisted that the other children should call her by this name at all times. They would knock on our door and ask, 'Is Flash coming out to play?' For a while she refused to answer to any other name.

Christmas was also a very happy time. Fiona, in particular, loved to anticipate the day. She would plan all her presents and cards meticulously. We always had stockings, and mince pies and drinks would be left out for Father Christmas and Rudolph. A few days before Christmas, we would decorate the tree together. We still use the angel which Fiona made one year. It has a bright pink cardboard body and a ping-pong ball face. It is one of my treasures now.

One Christmas, when Fi was six, I found she had taken all the decorations off the tree and dressed herself and Rebecca up in them. They had baubles and tinsel in their hair and were dancing around the room like fairies. They had such good fun that they did this every day and indeed every Christmas for a long time. I gave up artistically arranging the tree. They got much more fun out of using the decorations for their game.

When Fi was four and a half, she started part-time schooling at the local primary school. True to form, she was reluctant to be parted from me, but this time there was no choice and she soon settled down quite happily. She was an extremely bright child. I always received glowing reports and there were never any problems at this small, well-run, friendly school. She was still some- times quite nervous, particularly when she had to go back to school after a break. Given the chance, I know she would rather have been at home, but to the credit of her teachers, she did settle. Rebecca and John later fol- lowed her to this school.

During this period, my marriage finally ended. The children were seven, four and three years old respec- tively. I was given custody, but as I had no wish to deprive them of their father, who always loved them dearly, there were no rules about access. He was free to visit them whenever he wanted to and they could con- tact him as often as they wished. They were not easy times. I am sure they suffered from the break-up of our home, especially Fi, who was old enough to really understand what was happening. I know she missed her daddy tremendously and for a while her behaviour was very difficult. I was worried and disturbed by the split too and often didn't manage to cope very well with the after-effects.

Once, when I was trying to get the tangles out of Fiona's thick mop of curls, I must have been tugging too vigorously with the brush. She started to protest and cry loudly and then rounded on me, shrieking, 'Stop it. I'm going to live with Daddy. He wouldn't hurt me like you're doing.'

We both ended up in tears. The hair brushing was forgotten as we hugged and made up our quarrel.

I did my best to make the following years happy for the children. I was offered part-time work at Oakes Park, a school for children with physical disabilities. Rebecca and John were able to go to the school's nursery while I worked. This was a valuable experience as it taught them that disabled children were essentially the same as them. John used to envy them their wheelchairs and would often pinch one to scoot about in.

Because I worked, we were able to afford many enjoyable holidays and outings, starting with the Isle of Wight, in my ancient Mini, progressing to camping in the South of France and 'self-catering' in the Greek Islands and Tunisia.

On one day outing to London when the children were eight, five and four, we nearly lost Fiona. We were boarding the tube to take us to Trafalgar Square to see the pigeons. I had a rucksack on my back and held Rebecca and John firmly with each hand, Fi was walking just ahead. The train was by the platform as we came down the steps and she ran forwards and jumped on. She turned round to look for us as the automatic doors closed behind her. To my horror the train started to move slowly out of the station. I saw Fi mouth 'Mummy' as she disappeared from sight.

My imagination went into overdrive, as usual. 'My God! Eight years old and alone in London,' I whispered. Then, louder, 'Stop the train.'

But it was too late. It was already speeding up and well on its way out of the station. I grabbed the first guard I could find and explained to him what had happened.

'Don't panic,' he soothed, 'get on the next train and get off at the next stop. She will probably have got off there and be waiting for you.'

We followed his suggestion. It was the longest journey of my life. Sure enough, when we arrived at the station, there she was, waiting on the platform, beaming all over her face.

'An old lady talked to me, Mummy,' she said. 'I pretended that I was an American girl on holiday over here.' She then demonstrated her American accent.

'Oh Fiona!' we chorused. 'You are such a funny little girl. We thought you'd be scared stiff.'

But she hadn't been worried at all. She was such a

mixture, even then, frightened of going to school, petrified of doctors and dentists, yet completely unshaken at being alone in London at eight years of age. Later on in her life, she would walk among drug addicts and the criminal underworld without any fear at all.

There were many happy times to remember in those early childhood years. We have always loved music in our family. Fiona was quite a talented musician. She played the piano beautifully. It came to her very easily. She gained distinctions in all her piano exams quite effortlessly.

We all liked singing and when we were out in the car, we would sing at the top of our voices. 'Bring me oil in my lamp, keep me burning,' we would bellow as we bowled along.

In her final year at junior school, this love of singing led Fi to join the local church choir. We all attended this church for a while. Even at this age, Fi was exploring her spirituality. She decided by herself to become a member of the Church of England and was christened when she was eleven. None of the children had been christened or baptised at birth. I was so uncertain myself about religion that I felt it would be a great hypocrisy to undertake to bring my children up in a certain faith unless I intended to do so.

Fiona always searched for spiritual meaning in her life. In her last four years, she was never without her bible, hardly the image which springs to mind when one thinks of a prostitute. From my daughter I have learned never to judge by outward appearances. Many women in prostitution are portrayed by the media as 'slags' and 'tarts'. I know that I have been guilty in the past of judging these women as if they were some sort of different species. My experience has taught me differently.

'Never judge a person until you have walked a mile in their moccasins.' I often think of this old and very apt Indian saying now and apply it to my actions as much as possible.

In September 1987, Fiona began her secondary education at our local comprehensive. This school, taking pupils from eleven to eighteen, was comparatively small, with about eight hundred on the register at that time. Even so, it was an enormous jump from the family atmosphere of her junior school.

I am generally critical of these large impersonal comprehensives. Our children move from the security of their small, classroom-based junior schools to this more adult, curriculum-based environment at an early age. They spend a large proportion of their waking hours here, over one of the most difficult times of their lives – the turbulent adolescent period. We throw them in and they are left to develop their own survival tactics. Efforts are made to provide pastoral care but, with the best intentions in the world, these are often inadequate.

Many children, of course, cope well and even flourish in this situation, but there are others who flounder. These are often bright, sensitive young people, children like Fiona who, no matter how hard they try, just do not fit in. Believe me, these children suffer. You can usually spot them if you go and visit any comprehensive school. Some of them respond to their difficulties by withdrawing into themselves and simply enduring their school life. Others – and Fiona was one of these – try desperately hard to be accepted, to become one of the gang. But they remain on the outside. They are often jeered at mercilessly and may become the victims of bullying.

When Fi started at the school, its population was largely white, reflecting the nature of the suburb in which it was situated. Few children of ethnic origin lived in the neighbourhood. Most of the housing is privately owned. There are two small council estates in the area, both quite beautifully kept, with a waiting list of about ten years. This is not an area of deprivation, more an estate agent's dream: an ideal place in which to bring up your offspring.

Fi's first year at the school was uneventful. She settled in reasonably well. She had some close friends who had moved with her from primary school and they kept up their friendship.

On my own with the three children, I was struggling financially. Upkeep of the house and meeting the needs of three growing youngsters constantly drained my resources. I have always been a hopeless manager of my personal finances. No matter how much money I have, I spend it down to the last penny. I am one of those people for whom the credit card spells doom. I have had to suffer the shame of having my 'plastic' cut up under my nose by the bank manager.

Because I needed more cash, I increased my hours at Oakes Park. The work was only during the term, so the school holidays were not a problem. A very dear friend of our family, Silvia, looked after the children after school each day. Any guilt I had about leaving them was quickly dispelled. They loved going to Silvia's and her house became a second home for my three.

Our home life had quickly become stable again after the difficulties at the time of the divorce. There were no problems with the children. They were generally well behaved and happy.

Fiona remained an extremely active child. She was always either making up stories or writing plays. She would still from time to time immerse herself in fantasy. One Sunday we went to see the beautiful children's film, *E.T.* We all cried buckets, especially when the lovable alien, *E.T.*, leaves the boy, Michael, to return to his home in outer space. For a while Fi played at being Michael. She would ride up and down on her bicycle with the hood of her anorak up. These childish fantasies were happening less frequently, though, and she was growing up quite fast.

At around this time I decided to become a vegetarian, like many of my friends in the peace movement. The decision to try to live in harmony with the earth and its fellow creatures was quite personal. I never forced my views on the children or friends. My three made their own decisions. Rebecca was a vegetarian for about a year, but then her love of burgers overcame any idealistic principles. John lasted for about four years before he too succumbed. Fi remained a committed vegetarian until her death.

It was Fiona's vegetarianism which caused her the first problems at school. Being a child, she was not able to be as moderate in her viewpoint as I would have hoped. Also, being the girl she was, she just could not keep her opinions to herself. I am not sure exactly what started the trouble on this occasion, but I imagine that Fi may well have been expounding, at great length, her theories on cruelty to animals, etc., to her peers. Inevitably, it jarred. Before long a certain group of boys started to call her 'vegebugger'. What began as good-natured teasing quickly got out of hand. Fi had by now learned to keep her views on the subject to herself but the damage was done. Every time this group saw her, they would sing out at the top of their voices, 'Vegebugger, vegebugger.'

Fiona was very upset. Not wishing to make matters worse, I advised her to ignore them and it would stop, but of course it didn't and Fi became reluctant to go to school. At this stage I had to do something and so I decided to have a word with the mother of one of the boys. It wasn't an easy decision. I wasn't at all sure that it would do any good. I imagined the possibility of worse taunts such as 'Mummy's girl' being thrown at her. But Fiona was becoming distraught, and for the first time in ages didn't want to go to school to face her tormentors. Something had to be done.

Luckily the woman I spoke to was very sensible. She had a word with her son and the jeering quickly stopped. This mum told me afterwards that the boys simply hadn't realised that their teasing had gone a bit too far. I imagine that many other youngsters would have been able to cope; Fi couldn't. She just wasn't tough enough; never in her life was she able to ignore unkindness. Once this situation was resolved, she became happy to attend school once again and I hoped that lessons would be learned from her experience.

Fiona's second year was uneventful. She had excellent school reports and was very well behaved. She developed friendships with three of the quieter girls in her year. They were all starting to grow up and developing into young adults.

Music continued to play a big part in our lives. For a while Fi and I enjoyed the works of Andrew Lloyd Webber. I took all three children to see *Evita* in London. Fi was enthralled and became particularly interested in Eva Perón. Later she was to be fascinated by stories of people who died young: Marilyn Monroe, James Dean, Bob Marley and indeed Jesus Christ. Eva Perón was the first.

After our visit to see *Evita*, she warned me for the first time that she would not live to be old. I was struck cold with fear by her prediction.

'Please don't talk like that,' I begged. 'Stop being silly. Of course you won't die young.'

But later on in her life she often made this same chilling prediction, the last time with certainty, just two weeks before she died. I am now convinced that she really did know her fate. Following her death, many of her young friends came to me and said, 'Fiona knew she was going to die.'

After the flirtation with Lloyd Webber, Madonna and Michael Jackson took over as favourites. As always, Fi threw herself into these interests and soon she knew everything there was to know about them. Madonna was not a role model I would have chosen for my children, although I admired her musical talent.

Around this time, my mother had to go into hospital for surgery. One evening when the children and I were going to visit her, Fi spent a particularly long time getting ready. When she came down she was a vision.

Around that time, snood headwear, basically a knitted tube pulled on over the face and neck, was in vogue. Fi was wearing her snood as a skirt – a short, black, tight skirt. She was also wearing some black fishnet tights she had bought with her pocket money. The outfit was completed by a pair of high-heeled boots, which were supposed to be just for parties, and stunning bright red lipstick. I couldn't believe that she could dress so inappropriately and I shuddered to think what my mother's reaction would be. I pointed out to Fi that Granny's sense of respectability would be outraged. She would never upset her granny and so she went back upstairs and changed into something more suitable.

This was the first of many discussions to come over her appearance. She always loved dressing up and her choices often seemed outrageous to me. I wouldn't have minded what she wore to a nightclub, but on shopping trips to Morrisons I required a bit more conventionality. But Fi revelled in her appearance and, like many teenagers, found it hard to conform.

Fiona was also a fan of Michael Jackson. She learned all she could about his life, from his early years as a child star to his later obsessions with his health and appearance. There were some advantages to Jackson as a role model at that time, in particular his anti-drugs stance. During this phase – she was thirteen – Fi professed strong opposition to cigarettes and alcohol. Like her hero, she became very health conscious. She knew about Michael Jackson's obsession with clean air, and had heard the rumour that he slept in an oxygen tank. She asked her dad to get her a gas mask. He did, and to my amazement, she actually wore it out to our local shops in an effort to avoid breathing in the pollutants from the traffic on the adjacent busy main road. Her schoolfriends thought she was crazy.

This incident perfectly illustrates what she was like. She passionately believed in her principles and would act on them, even at the risk of being ridiculed. But then, when the inevitable happened and she was teased and laughed at, she couldn't stand it. It was often done very unkindly. She seemed to be trapped. She was unable to compromise or to be more moderate in her views, and completely incapable of keeping quiet about them. She could not see that her extreme behaviour was often counter-productive and simply made her a figure of fun, someone to giggle and gossip about.

It was in the third year, starting in September 1989, that Fiona started to have real problems. She started to make excuses to get out of going to school, frequently complaining of feeling unwell in the mornings. I would try to jolly her along. She told me that she was never part of the group which seemed to be having fun. She and her three friends were apparently not in the 'in' crowd. This upset her a lot. She also seemed to be the target for a lot of petty, unkind teasing.

She told me about one incident in the classroom. She had walked in and, for once, was greeted in a friendly fashion. She had thought to herself, 'Oh good, they're going to be nice to me today.' But then one of the girls walked over to her, unzipped her pencil case and tipped its contents all over the floor. This was accompanied by raucous shrieks of laughter from the other girls. Fiona said that she simply picked up her pencils and tried very hard not to cry.

There were many small incidents like this. They always happened when there was no adult supervision, often when the pupils were waiting in the classroom for the teacher to arrive, or as they moved between sites.

On another occasion, the boys in her class made a list of the girls they would most like to kiss. Fi's name was at the bottom and they made sure that she saw it. At the time she was wearing a fixed brace on her teeth and probably wasn't very kissable. She came home and sobbed for a whole evening, inconsolable.

She also managed to get on the wrong side of one of the older girls, and this episode had far-reaching consequences. It started quite simply. Fi and some of her friends went into the girls' toilets and discovered some of the older girls smoking in there. This was at the height of her obsession with Michael Jackson. Unable to keep quiet, Fi made a show of coughing and spluttering, and said loudly to her friends, 'We'll all get lung cancer from passive smoking at this school.' Unfortunately one of the girls was a fifteen-year-old with a hard reputation to maintain. From that day onwards, this girl and her cronies made Fiona's life hell, not just in school but out of it as well. They called her a slag and jeered loudly at her whenever they saw her. She became very frightened of going anywhere on her own in case she bumped into this girl.

She once was slapped very hard across the face on the school bus. 'I went dizzy and it made my ears ring, Mum,' she told me, crying.

I asked some of her friends who had been on the bus whether she had provoked this attack. They assured me that she had done nothing to deserve the blow, but had simply been sitting quietly.

At this point I felt it was time the school intervened so I went in to see Fi's year tutor and also the person in charge of pastoral care. It was suggested that Fiona should come out of class for forty minutes, once a week, for guidance from her tutor on how to deal with the bully.

She was absolutely mortified. 'I haven't done any-thing wrong,' she complained, 'and I'm the one having to come out of class. Everyone is going to think it's my fault. Why don't they expel the person who's making my life a misery. They haven't said anything to her at all.'

In fact the older girl was spoken to but to no positive effect, as she persisted in her behaviour towards Fi, if anything with renewed fervour.

Over the next few weeks Fiona started to feel unwell or have headaches on the days she should have been receiving her lessons on how to cope with the bullying, so this was a non-starter. In despair, I decided to attempt to resolve the situation myself. With my ever-lasting faith in the human race, I said to Fi that this girl couldn't be all nasty, and that maybe things had just got out of hand. We decided to go to the shop where she worked and see if we could have a word with her.

Choosing a moment when there was no one else around, I said, to the girl, 'Look, Fiona is very miserable and frightened of you and your friends. She's also a lot younger than you. She didn't mean to upset you in the first place, so why not make friends and get on with your lives without bothering each other.'

We waited eagerly for a smile from the girl and her reassurance that it would finish. I shall never forget the cold, hard glare on her face as she refused my offer. Neither shall I forget Fiona's misery on the way home.

'I told you what she was like, Mum,' she cried. 'Now you can see what I've had to put up with.'

Fi was now frightened of travelling on the school bus and I started to take her to school myself in the mornings. After school, she would do her best never to be on her own as she made her way to Silvia's.

There is no point in my blaming or trying to harm the school now. I am trying to give a true account of what happened to Fiona; her school years are part of that account. She was very badly affected by her experiences at this time. Perhaps more could have been done, but the school was no better or worse than any of the comprehensives when it comes to dealing with issues of this nature. I feel that all secondary schools lack sufficient resources to deal with the problems which children like

Fiona come up against. The school does now have in practice a very good anti-bullying policy and during a recent inspection was praised for its low incidence of bullying.

It was during this deeply unhappy period that Fiona met Elroy, a black man of thirty-two and a Rastafarian. This was probably the key event which finally and irrevocably 'blew it' for her at school.

For some time it had been clear that she was developing a strong social conscience. In her history lessons she had been learning about the slave trade and apartheid. She was visibly upset at the treatment of black people and I would find her weeping all the way through *Uncle Tom's Cabin*.

The issues surrounding racism were to play a prominent part in Fiona's life. It was her dismay at historic racial injustices which led her actively to seek out the company of black people. It was as if she wanted to dissociate herself from the actions of her ancestors and somehow make up for all that cruelty and unhappiness. At the time, I thought that this was normal behaviour for a sensitive teenager, but as usual, she threw herself into her latest interest with more enthusiasm than most.

I remember very clearly when Fiona met Elroy. She was fourteen. It was a Saturday afternoon and she had gone into the city centre to do some shopping.

Fi had a habit of giving her money away to down-and-outs. She was particularly fond of a small Irish alcoholic who regularly received part of her pocket money. This was exasperating but it was useless to tell her that it would only be spent on drink. She used to feel so sorry for these men; she told me it was the only thing she could do to help.

This particular Saturday afternoon Fi was sitting in the Peace Gardens, an area in the town centre, where her Irish friend sometimes sat, when she met Vernon. Vernon was a middle-aged black South African. He was also a hopeless alcoholic. I was to meet Vernon a few times. On the rare occasions that I saw him sober, he was a gentle, kind and sensitive man. When drunk, he became an aggressive, violent, rampaging creature who scared the wits out of me. I was told that in his youth he had been offered a place at Balliol College in Oxford, but any prospects he had were ruined by his unconquerable addiction to alcohol.

While Vernon was telling Fiona about his life in South Africa, they were joined by Elroy, who was a passing acquaintance of his.

Elroy was Fi's first introduction to the Rastafarian culture. My daughter was instantly smitten.

When she came home, she told me all about him and

that she had arranged to meet him in town the next day. Alarm bells rang in my head. What could this man want with my daughter, so much younger than him?

Fi's reply to my questioning did nothing to reassure me. 'He's in trouble, Mum,' she said. 'He desperately needs money. I said I could give him £5 out of my savings.'

'What sort of trouble?' I asked. 'He shouldn't be asking young girls for money. It's not right, Fi, I'm definitely not happy about this at all.'

Later on I learned that Elroy was being charged with indecently exposing himself. Apparently some girls had been laughing and staring at him on the top deck of a bus. Annoyed by their persistent giggling, he had unzipped his trousers in order to shut them up. This had the desired effect, but unfortunately for Elroy, they told the bus driver and he was arrested as he stepped off the bus.

As I got to know more about Elroy, I realised that it was his fondness for marijuana, which caused most of his problems. Indeed this was probably why he had asked Fiona if she had any money to spare.

At the time I knew none of this. I did not want Fiona to keep her appointment with him because I was suspicious of his motives in wanting to meet a girl eighteen years younger than himself and also because he had asked her for money. It seemed to me to be completely inappropriate.

Fiona, however, thought differently. The more we discussed it, the more determined she became to go ahead and meet him. She harangued me all that evening and started up again the next morning. It was soon obvious that no matter how much I threatened, bribed, blackmailed or wheedled, she was not going to listen to me. I recognised my powerlessness and decided to compromise.

'Let me take you down in the car then,' I said. 'You can introduce me to him and it will set my mind at rest.'

I was pleased when Fi agreed to this and we set off in the car for town. When we reached the meeting place, Elroy wasn't there. I breathed a sigh of relief. Fi was really disappointed and asked if we could hang on for a bit longer. We waited for five minutes and I was just about to set off for home when he appeared.

Elroy was of medium height. His dreadlocked hair was tied back in a ponytail with bands in the African colours of red, gold and green. I found his face quite striking. To me he seemed to have all the beauty and nobility of his proud African ancestors. His black skin was smooth and flawless and when he spoke his big brown eyes shone.

If he was surprised that Fiona had brought her mother along to meet him, he didn't show it. He jumped into the back of the car and started chatting. My initial impression was of an intelligent, thoughtful man. I could see why Fiona was attracted to him. He displayed a lot of insight and a great capacity for philosophical thought.

Nevertheless I told him I was concerned that Fi wanted to give him money and asked him why he needed it. He was embarrassed and insisted that he didn't want her money.

'I am in a bit of trouble,' he told me, 'but I will be all right.'

We then got on to the subject of drugs, and in particular, marijuana. Elroy expounded at great length on its qualities. He called it either 'ganja' or 'draw'.

'This drug,' he told me, 'is a holy herb. When you smoke it, it clears your mind. It helps you to meditate and it brings you closer to God. You can read about it in the bible. It grew on the grave of King Solomon. It is such a powerful herb that you should be baking it into cakes and giving it to your children.'

'But it's illegal,' I protested. 'And why do you need a drug to get close to God?'

I couldn't agree with Elroy at all on this subject, but I could see that Fiona was impressed. Eventually he left us. I had chided him again for asking Fi for money and made sure that he was aware of how young she was, much to her embarrassment.

In the car on the way home we continued our conversation about drugs. Apparently they had been learning about them in social studies at school. I could tell that Fi's stand was wavering.

'Not everybody thinks that smoking marijuana is wrong, Mum,' she told me. 'Our teacher told us that there is this religion which believes that smoking it is good for you. It's the Rastafarian religion. Elroy is a Rastafarian. They believe in peace and love and in being vegetarians, just like you.'

'But what about its bad effects?' I asked. 'What's more, you mustn't forget that it's illegal to use it in this country, and you could get into a lot of trouble if you have it in your possession. Don't get involved with any drugs, please, Fi. You really don't need them, they'll only mess you up.'

Over the years to come we would have many conversations like this one. Nothing I have experienced during those years has made me waver from this viewpoint. I watched helplessly while Fiona succumbed to the temptation to use marijuana heavily, and also while she tried a range of other illegal drugs.

I know without a doubt that she would never have been able to sell her body on the streets of Doncaster, unless she had dulled her mind to the reality of her situation by the use of drugs.

After this meeting with Elroy, I suggested to Fiona that it was not a good idea to see him again. I was very concerned both about his attitude to marijuana and the age difference between them. The colour of his skin was not important to me.

I was soon to realise, however, that Fiona was still

meeting him, usually in town on a Saturday afternoon. She became obsessed with Africa and would frequently tie her hair back like his with red, gold and green pony-tail bands. Elroy had also told her that black people used coconut oil on their hair, so of course Fi was not happy until she had bought some and tried it out on her curls.

Tongues soon started to wag in all-white Totley when word got around that Fiona was associating with a black man. Once I was walking home with her when a group of young people congregated outside the video shop yelled across the road at her: 'Nigger lover.'

I was furious and was all for going across the road to deliver one of my anti-racist lectures to these young men.

Fi stopped me. 'It's no use, Mum. They won't listen to you. They'll only laugh and I'll really get it when I go to school.'

Recognising the truth of what she was saying, I desisted, but I was very angry.

Fiona's dreadful unhappiness at school was becoming apparent. This association with Elroy unfortunately estranged her from the three girls who had been her only allies. They were lovely girls and I know for certain that at least one of them had also been very unhappy there. They were unable to help Fiona at this point. They were much more worldly-wise and possibly more aware of the dangers that such a friendship might bring.

I know they cared for her but they could do nothing.

Round about this time Fi was involved in doing the Duke of Edinburgh's award scheme. It was a welcome break for her as it got her away from the classroom where she was suffering so dreadfully. In order to gain the award the young people had to demonstrate their survival skills on a camping trip. Fiona was able to do this with two of the girls in her year who never joined in with the general unkindness and teasing.

Before the trip itself they had a practice run in our garden. Fi and her two friends each contributed £5 to their living expenses. I expected to see them heating up beans and frying eggs on their stove out in the open, so I was highly amused when, on the second evening, a young man on a moped with Pizza Hut emblazoned all over it arrived with pizza for these three intrepid adventurers.

On the actual trip, they camped on a very small site, North Lees, in Derbyshire. I had presumed that they would be supervised; they were, after all, only fourteen. I was consequently dismayed to learn that on the evening they were there, a large group of university students was also camping on the site. During the night the students returned from the pub and invited the schoolgirls to join them. Fiona and some of the more adventurous girls from another year group did so and marijuana 'spliffs' were passed around. I believe that this was Fi's first experience with this or any drug. I was extremely annoyed that it should happen on an activity sanctioned by the school but, in my view, not properly supervised.

I still believe that to expect most adolescents to behave sensibly is to expect too much. To my mind there has never been a worse time to be young.

When Fiona returned to school after this camping trip, things went from bad to worse. After her murder, the teacher who had provided home education during the period when I could no longer get her into school gave me a piece of work Fi had written. It describes very poignantly her misery at the time. It is included here.

'Look at that red, gold and green band in her hair', said Jason's loud voice from the back of the classroom. 'I know,' commented Wanda loudly. 'She feel seh she a rasta'. Next came the sound of laughter. That was one of the sounds I dreaded the most . . . In reality only two or three people were laughing but to me it seemed like the whole class was mocking me. The sound surrounded me and made my head spin. I shut my eyes and took a deep breath. The air smelled musty like the old curtains that attempted to cover the windows and like the ancient-looking books in the dusty cupboards. Opening my eyes again, after the laughter had subsided, I glanced at my watch. Five minutes left until the start of registration.

Five minutes – a twelfth of an hour – three hundred seconds. It was just too long. I began to stand up. Then I heard something else I didn't want to hear. Wanda had just said something about Bob Marley. That meant I was in trouble. Whenever Bob Marley was mentioned, someone was talking about me. I sat back down and tried to look as if I hadn't heard what they were saying. Jason was walking towards the front of the classroom. I could hear his voice getting louder as he approached. I turned and pretended to talk to the girl next to me, hoping he wouldn't notice the anxiety on my face but it was too late. He had grabbed a handful of my knotted hair and tugged it so that I was leaning backwards over my chair, looking up at him. 'Is wha' dis den?' he asked 'Dis you natty dread?' I felt my eyes starting to water. I couldn't let him see that he was upsetting me. 'Yeah,' I replied. 'Well why's it look dat way deh? A no locks dat.' I wanted to shout at him. Hundreds of words were flying round inside my head but they refused to come out of my mouth so I ignored him and pretended I wasn't bothered. I wished he would go away and leave me alone. It seemed as if the whole class was staring at me. The voices of all the people in the classroom had turned into one – a deafening buzz that confused me and made me dizzy. My eyes were open but I wasn't looking at anything and I could no longer hear what Jason was saying. His voice was just a jumble of sounds. I had turned myself off. If I couldn't hear them, they couldn't upset me. Suddenly the loud ringing of the morning registration bell brought me back to life. Everyone was sitting down quietly as the teacher walked into the room. For fifteen minutes I was safe. I relaxed in my chair and thought about my birthday which was the next day. My brother and sister had got a big present for me and I hadn't a clue what it was. Just as I began to forget about school we were told to get off to our next lesson. A great surge of teenagers rushed to the door, laughing with each other. I waited until the last few had gone before I got up and left. I was too scared to join in with the pushing and shoving. The other kids were always telling me about trying to join in with them and I had given up the idea of having a laugh with everyone else.

I walked to the French room carefully avoiding eye contact with anyone. It wasn't just my class that I was afraid of. It was the whole school. The French room was locked and everybody was standing outside the toilets which were opposite the classroom. I put my bag on top of the cupboard and sat down next to it. Gina was mouthing off at every quiet kid that came near her, about wearing the wrong clothes. I looked at the trainers on my feet. When I first got them even the boys who picked on me asked me where I got them from, but now they were old and I couldn't afford any more for about a month. I dangled my bag in front of my feet so that she couldn't see them. Anna, Sophie and Maria were standing by the cupboard. They had been my best friends until a few weeks ago. When everyone found out about my boyfriend they had all presumed that I was either easy or a drug addict. I smiled at the three girls. They smiled back and then got on with their conversation.

The bell rang for dinner time. I had arranged to meet Sophie and Anna for lunch and when I reached the entrance hall they were half way up the queue. For a dreadful moment I thought I was on my own but then I saw them waving and telling me to jump the queue. I stood with them, not knowing what to say. They talked about television programmes that I didn't watch, music I didn't listen to, films I'd never seen and places where I'd never been. I began to realise how far apart I was from the people that used to be my friends. The things they were talking about were to me uninteresting and childish and the things I wanted to say would have shocked them. We sat down to eat and Sophie and Anna kept talking – this time about some friends of theirs that I didn't know. At first I had been pleased to have some company but I started to wish I hadn't come with them. I felt sure they were talking about things I didn't know about deliberately. Sophie made a strange remark and they both roared with laughter. 'You what?' I asked, puzzled. 'Private joke,' said Sophie. I was obviously not going to be let in on it so I nodded and smiled but really I felt like crying. These girls had been my best friends. We used to go to town together and talk about everything. We had joked together about how terrible we were at football and bought each other things back from our holidays. Now we were acting

*like strangers. As soon as I finished my lunch I said good-
bye to them and left the room.*

*I walked outside and up the drive to the other building.
As I came to the road between the two buildings I saw
Gina and Lucy standing at the 'smokers' wall' so I
changed direction and headed for the main entrance to
the building but when I got a bit further I noticed Wendy
with her boyfriend Roy. All of a sudden the idea of going
to my English lesson seemed too much to handle. I knew
what would happen already. I would sit next to Sophie,
Maria and Anna who would get on with their work quietly
while the rest of the girls got chased around the classroom by the boys. Anna, Sophie and Maria didn't mind
being left out of the action. They were perfectly happy to
talk to each other but I wished I could join in with the
other girls while they messed around with the boys, but to
be in their gang you had to be loud and enjoy picking on
people and I wasn't like that. I waited until Wendy and
Roy had gone and walked down the road to go home.*

*I woke up on my birthday feeling fed up. I pleaded with
my mother not to make me go to school but it didn't work.
At quarter to nine I was sitting in the classroom again,
trying not to look at anyone or get noticed by anyone. I
remembered Angela's birthday a week ago. Everyone in
the class had given her a card and most of them a present
as well. Nobody in the room even knew it was my birthday.
The boys at the back of the classroom were trying to kiss
all the girls. The girls kept saying a line out of a TV*

advert every time someone asked them something. I had been the first one to say it but I was told 'No, you're not good,' by Roy so I shut up. Now, a few weeks later everyone was saying it and apparently Roy had started it.

Our first lesson was music and we went into another classroom to watch a video. As everybody gathered round the television I found myself sitting near the big gang of girls. Angela, one of the quieter ones, said 'Hi Fiona'. I smiled at her. Then some of her friends said hello to me but when Louisa, the leader of the gang, saw me she said loudly 'Bye Fiona'. And laughed. The other girls who were really a bit scared of her copied her. 'Yeah, bye Fiona,' they all said. I moved my chair away slightly and sat on my own. All the way through the video the girls were talking and giggling. I wanted so much to join in with them but even when they let me talk to them they just made me feel stupid. They wouldn't let me in on their jokes and when they all cracked up for no apparent reason I just pretended to laugh but really I felt left out and miserable. Sometimes I would play a joke on Anna and they would all give me a look that said 'How can you be so immature. That's not even funny,' but another time I would see them do exactly the same thing and go on like it was the funniest joke ever invented.

I hated lessons but I hated breaks even more. Everyone had at least two really good friends who they would sit with and talk to. I had two groups of girls who would let me tag along behind them. I used to just wander around the school on my own but now there were too many people that didn't like me and I felt safer with someone else. This time though I was on my own. Wanda, Lucy and Gina walked into the classroom where I was sitting. I wanted to crawl under the table and hide but I knew I couldn't. There was nobody in the classroom for me to hide behind or pretend to be talking to. I sat, looking at the floor waiting for something to happen. To my surprise Wanda came up to me and said 'Hi Fiona. What you doin'?'

'Nothing.' I replied. 'Just thinking'.

'What, about this new boyfriend of yours? What's he like?' she asked. I described him to her. Then Gina butted in, 'I bet he smokes ganga innit?' I just nodded. I didn't want to have to talk about that. People had already got the idea that I was on hard drugs and I didn't want to give them more reason to talk than they already had. Gina had gone out with a black man who had treated her really badly. He was always beating her up and she now thought that all black men were the same as him.

She started asking me what he had done to me. 'Nothing,' I replied.

'Didn't he even kiss you?' she asked. I nodded my head.

'What else did he do?' I insisted there was nothing but she wouldn't believe me. She kept asking if we had done certain things and I didn't understand what she meant. I blushed and they took that to mean yes. They laughed, but it was a friendly laugh, not the nasty laugh that I was used to. I talked to them until the bell rang and they went *off to their separate lessons after promising not to tell anyone what we had been saying.*

I managed to get through the art lesson knowing that I had just been talking to the three 'hardest' girls in my year, but at dinner time I was back on my own again. I decided not to go into dinner. People in the queue would be pushing each other around and being loud, and I was terrified of going in there on my own. As I walked to my classroom people I hardly knew kept making comments as they passed me. At first the comments were just things like 'Naughty girl' and 'Have a nice time, did you?' but as I got to the classroom I saw all the boys from my class, a lot of Wanda's friends and the gang of girls led by Louisa. I wanted to turn round and come back to the room when they had gone but then they would tease me even more for being scared of them so I walked towards them, trying to look confident despite my heart beating at twice its usual rate. I took a deep breath as I approached them. 'Excuse me,' I whispered. Nobody moved. I tried to walk through the crowd but when I got to the centre they started shouting at me. I turned round to walk back to the library where there would be a teacher and someone grabbed one of my locks. Then they suddenly let go. 'God, what's she got in her hair?' they shouted.

'Smells like coconut,' someone replied. Everybody was laughing and shouting. As I ran to the door I heard someone calling after me, 'See ya, nigger lover.'

I ran out of the school and halfway down the road. I

didn't stop running until I reached the main road. I crossed over and waited for the bus to come. Later on, sitting in my bedroom, I realised that I could never go back to school again. I never told my mother what had happened that day but she knew that I couldn't face having everybody laughing at me. When I was quiet and sensible I had been teased about that, and when I started to act like the other girls I was still teased. I had tried to fit in but I couldn't and I knew they would never leave me to be myself so that day I left school for good.

Oh that we could bring back time and change things. I torture myself now that I didn't do enough to help her. I used to think that she was over-reacting to her problems. I don't know why she was unable to tell the teachers at school the extent of her misery. Maybe her behaviour did make her seem a bit of an oddity; no doubt it contributed to her position. All the same, no child should ever be frightened to go to school, no matter how eccentric or different they are. Fiona didn't deserve her treatment and was terribly hurt and undermined by it. Its effects stayed with her for the rest of her life.

The dreadful taunting and jeering because she was naive enough to tell some of the girls about her friendship with Elroy, described in her essay, was a huge blow to her self-esteem. I am convinced that this was a major factor in making her vulnerable to the pimp, Zebbi, who ultimately took advantage of her innocence and gave her to her murderer.

The immediate result was that Fiona knew she couldn't make it in that environment. No matter how hard she tried she could never fit in. This was to have serious consequences.

The culmination of all this misery was quite dramatic. One morning Fi came down from breakfast looking really miserable and clutching her stomach.

'Mum, I feel really sick,' she moaned.

'Oh come on, Fi,' I chided. 'You can't stay off school again. You're having more days off than you're going in.'

'But I'm not well,' she insisted, and the tears weren't far off.

In the past I had given her the benefit of the doubt when she complained of feeling unwell, but now it was happening more and more often. At the time I had been called to do jury service and I have to admit my mind was also occupied with that. If only I'd realised then quite how bad things were for her at school.

'Go in,' I insisted, 'and if you still don't feel well, I'll get someone to come and pick you up and bring you home.'

She trudged reluctantly back up the stairs.

I carried on with the usual morning tasks associated with getting myself ready for the day and three children off to school. Fi seemed to be rather a long time in coming back downstairs.

'Come on, Fi,' I shouted a few times. When there was no response I went upstairs to hurry her along. I found her in the bathroom. She had an empty packet of paracetamol tablets in her hand.

'My God, what have you done? You idiot, Fi,' I screamed at her in fright. 'How many have you taken? Don't you know these are deadly?'

I grabbed the packet out of her hand. I couldn't remember how full the box had been.

'Come on, Fi,' I said more gently as I tried to get a hold of myself. 'Tell me. How many have you taken? You don't really want to die, do you?'

She looked a bit scared. 'I don't want to die but I can't go to school.'

'OK,' I said. 'You're not going to school. Tell me. How many have you taken?'

'I'm not sure, Mum,' was the answer. 'I think there were about twelve in the box.'

By now Rebecca and John were wondering what was going on. I tried to reassure them that Fiona was all right. I was panicking though. I knew that paracetamol could cause irreversible damage to the liver and that people had died by inadvertently overdosing on quite small amounts. I rang my GP and spoke to the receptionist.

'Take her to casualty straight away,' I was advised.

The nearest casualty unit which was open was at the Northern General, a hospital right across the other side of town. I got everybody into the car and, after dropping an unhappy Rebecca and John off at their school, Fiona and I made our way across town.

For a while we were both quiet in the car. Then I tried to get her to talk about it.

'I don't want to die, Mum,' was all she would say. 'I hate school. I'm so unhappy there. They're all horrible to me.'

I felt hopeless then. I seemed to be unable to do anything about the situation. A change of school now seemed our only option and I decided that we would have to consider this urgently.

As soon as we arrived at the casualty unit we were taken into a small side ward. Fiona was seen fairly quickly by one of the doctors.

'She will be all right, won't she?' I pleaded.

'We don't know,' was the calm answer. 'We'll give her a drink which will make her sick, and then we'll have to take some blood. This will tell us the level of paracetamol she's absorbed and whether she's in any danger from it.'

Fiona was told to undress and given a white hospital gown to put on. She was then given a glass full of a liquid which she had to drink. A nurse watched to make sure she drank it all. She looked very pathetic and I was close to tears. I sat with her holding the bowl as we waited for her to be sick. Fiona always hated being sick.

'You'll not do this again, will you?' I said to her as we waited. It wasn't long before she was vomiting in the bowl. I held her until she had finished.

In due course the blood test came back. To my relief Fi hadn't absorbed enough paracetamol to do any lasting damage.

The nurse told us that Fiona wouldn't be allowed to go home until she had been seen by a psychiatrist. 'It's hospital policy when anyone takes an overdose,' she explained to me.

Fiona was allowed to get dressed and then we sat and waited. By now it was around lunch-time. After about an hour in the waiting room we were told that an appointment had been made for Fiona to see someone from the adolescent psychiatric unit at 2 p.m. I asked if it would be all right if we took a walk and perhaps had a drink at the WVS canteen. I was told this would be OK.

We found the WVS and as by now we were both hungry, we decided to have cheese sandwiches. We were both feeling a little better and I was thinking that maybe this psychiatrist would be able to help. No sooner had we eaten our sandwiches than I noticed that Fi had gone a deathly white colour.

'I'm going to be sick,' she gasped.

I couldn't see where the toilets were and there wasn't time to ask. I rushed her outside and she threw up violently all over the entrance to the WVS. Why on earth hadn't they warned her not to have anything to eat, I fumed to myself. This was adding insult to injury. I was going to apologise to someone for the mess and then I thought, 'To hell with it. They should have told Fi that the emetic would still be working.'

People were staring at us as if Fi was a drunk or something. So I put my arm around her and we hurried away as fast as we could to find the adolescent unit.

After a short wait we were ushered into a small room with some easy chairs and a contrived atmosphere of informality. The psychiatrist who had been assigned to us was a young man, tall and thin with floppy hair and piercing eyes. He started asking Fi some questions. I could tell that she was antagonised by him. I don't know how it happened but somehow we were sidetracked on to the subject of racism. I felt very awkward. Why were we talking about racism? Fiona had taken the para-cetamol to get out of going to school. Why were we going off on her hobby horse? We seemed to be getting nowhere.

'Perhaps it would be better if I wasn't here,' I suggested, thinking that maybe a nurse could come in and chaperone.

'No, Mum,' Fi shrieked, 'you can't leave me on my own with this white man.'

I wondered if he thought she was mad, but he didn't seem too perturbed.

Looking back now, I am appalled at what I saw as the lack of expertise shown by this young man. He was supposed to be used to dealing with teenagers. It seemed to me that he didn't show any warmth or sympathy to this girl who, just a few hours previously, had been gulping down paracetamol because she dreaded going to school.

It was another opportunity missed. We were to have another couple of appointments with this psychiatrist but they were as unproductive as the first. I almost had to drag Fiona down to see him. In the end, I couldn't see any point in it.

On discharging us, he wrote to my GP. I asked for and received a copy of his letter. Not once were Fiona's fears about school mentioned. He said in his letter that I was dealing with Fiona's problems by distancing myself from the situation and that Fiona was 'raising the stakes in order to antagonise her mother'.

In retrospect I realise I should have asked to see someone else, or this should have been suggested to me. I hadn't had a lot of faith in psychiatry before this episode. Now I had none at all. I decided I would have to help Fiona as well as I could by myself.

I know that Fiona's desperate misery at school had lowered her self-esteem. The incident described in her essay had pushed her to make this half-hearted attempt at suicide, this cry for help. There are a number of measures that might have helped, if taken at an earlier stage – a change of tutor group, for example, or even a different school. Unfortunately, by the time I realised how serious the situation was, it was too late, and Fiona was scarred mentally by her experiences. There was no way she was going to return to school.

At this stage the school itself made an effort to help. They decided to home in on Fiona's expressed hatred of injustice, especially those issues concerned with racism. She had voiced some fairly strong opinions on how history was being taught. She would fume about children being told that Christopher Columbus discovered America, 'as if the native Indians didn't exist!'

The 'great' British Empire was something else she would become heated about. To Fi's mind there was nothing at all 'great' about invading other people's countries and forcing our civilisation upon their already well-developed cultures.

Later on, as she mixed more with the Rastafarians, she would expound upon 'the great white lie', namely the fact that Jesus is always portrayed as a white man.

'In the bible,' she would point out, 'it says that "his hair was woolly like a lamb". He must have been black with hair like that,' she told me triumphantly.

'Well, I really don't mind what colour he was,' I would reply.

'That's because you haven't ever been put down because of the colour of your skin.'

The school thought it would be a good idea for Fiona

to do some work around this theme. It was suggested that she should look at how history was being taught in class and determine whether these and other issues were being presented fairly. It was basically a very good idea and Fi was keen to have a go.

One of the peripatetic teachers, who helped children from ethnic origins to integrate, was to help her to set up the project. This young man was extremely personable and likeable. By this time I was unable to persuade Fi into school at all, so he visited us both at home. After we had discussed the idea, he told me that he had a friend who was much more versed in this area than he was. His name was Joah and it was arranged that they would both visit us the following week.

Sure enough, the next week, they arrived at our house and Joah was introduced. He was a Rastafarian. His hair hung in black dreadlocks down to his waist. He wore the uniform crocheted cap in red, gold and green. He spoke with a Jamaican accent and his speech often seemed to slur. I was beginning to recognise the signs of a user of marijuana and I knew that Joah was actually 'stoned'.

The usually vociferous Fiona was struck dumb. She was completely enthralled and unable to open her mouth at all during this visit.

I am afraid that Joah put my back up immediately. I'm sure the feeling was mutual. To be fair to him, he must have wondered why a white girl should be so concerned about the teaching of black history. Maybe he saw it as yet another incidence of white people 'taking over'. He was filled with hatred for white society. He quoted me the slave trade, apartheid, the great white lie and all the other injustices meted out to the black race.

'I am really sorry,' I heard myself saying yet again, 'but I wasn't there at the time. You can't go on for ever blaming present-day society for yesterday's mistakes. We've tried to make it up to you – especially in Sheffield, where we've tried really hard to right some of these wrongs.'

But he was having none of it.

I tried to joke. 'You're not the only people to be discriminated against. What about me? I'm female and Irish.'

But Joah didn't want to know. I don't think he was interested in helping a white family. There was no way we could make this work.

I gave him a lift into town afterwards. I tried to make conversation with him about ordinary events not connected with racism, but I had the feeling that he couldn't wait to get away from me.

I was very disappointed at this meeting. Subsequently Fi's project was dropped. Fi herself never mentioned it again and the idea was shelved. To this day I don't know why it was not followed up. Nobody – not the ethnic minorities teacher, not Joah, not even the school – ever contacted us to see if it was going ahead. I myself did nothing about it. I was so dismayed by the appearance of Joah on the scene that I couldn't see any point. I thought I would be labelled as difficult and uncooperative if I objected to him. I was also beginning to feel extremely depressed and hopeless about the whole situation.

During this period, although I was not aware of it at the time, Fi was regularly visiting Elroy at his flat. Even if I'd known, I wasn't in a position to stop her: I couldn't force her back to school and, as I was working full time, there was no one to supervise her. Besides, after all her unhappiness, she felt that in Elroy she'd found someone to love her for herself.

As she was not attending school, we received a visit from the educational welfare officer (EWO). I don't think he knew what to make of Fiona. By this time she had absorbed more of the Rastafarian philosophy, including the belief that present-day Western society was essentially corrupt. She told him that she was avoiding school in order to remain free of its influence. I'm sure this must have been one of the most novel excuses for non-attendance that the EWO had ever heard. Nevertheless, following his visit, we made one more attempt to get her back into school.

We were summoned into the office of the deputy head, a teacher of the old-school disciplinary type who has since retired. I don't think Fi opened her mouth once during this interview.

'Now we'll have no more of this nonsense,' she was told. 'You're to come straight back into school. If you don't, your mother's name will be put on the list for the authorities and she'll have to pay a hefty fine.'

Poor Fi. How I wish that we had all dug much deeper into the reasons for her reluctance to go to school. She was a very bright child and to my knowledge she always behaved impeccably. Why are some children so unkind to others? How many more Fionas are enduring these inhuman jungles we call school?

Following this interview, Fi returned to her class for one day, and then again refused to attend. It was decided at this stage that the only answer now would be a complete change. We visited all the schools within a reasonable distance and eventually selected another comprehensive with a good reputation and a nice mix of pupils, situated about six miles from our home.

I myself was under extreme pressure. Although I always enjoyed my job, the demands it made on me were considerable. The house we were living in required never-ending maintenance and had a large garden which I never managed to get topside of. Job, house, garden, financial problems, plus three growing children were proving an enormous strain.

I was desperately concerned for Fiona, but I didn't know how I could help her. Her increasing infatuation with the Rastafarian community and my growing suspicions that she was starting to take drugs created a difficult atmosphere in our house. We would have ferocious arguments and I could tell that Rebecca and, to a lesser extent, John were beginning to be affected by our unhappiness. To try and give us all a break from some of these problems, I decided to splash out on a holiday. Fi was really keen to go to Africa, and we thought Tunisia would be worth a try.

We went during the half-term break in October 1990. The children were fourteen, eleven and ten respectively. It turned out to be the first holiday as a family which we didn't enjoy. Basically, we took our problems with us. I was appalled at the poverty of the local people. I felt ashamed to be living in the luxury of the hotel, while outside, small children begged and stole to survive. We had towels, clothes and money stolen from us. I wasn't angry about it: the people were so poor, I felt it was almost justified and I didn't blame them in the least. There was no welfare state here to protect these children. Most of them received no schooling. They had to earn their keep selling oranges to the tourists on the beaches. They did what they had to in order to survive.

True to form, Fi couldn't settle for a holiday lazing on the beach or swimming in the hotel pool. She was impossible to contain and ruined the holiday for the rest of us. She struck up a number of friendships with these street urchins. While John, Rebecca and I played tennis and swam in the hotel pool, she would slip away to the beach to talk to these native children of Tunisia. At times I was worried sick: they would invite her back to their homes to meet their families and she would disappear for hours. She would reappear, quite unconcerned, with small gifts they had given her. If she had told me where she was going, I would have forbidden it, but of course she never did.

As it was, I imagined her being sold in the white slave trade. It was a standing joke with the Tunisian men. Every day one of them would approach me and, gesturing at either Fi or Rebecca, laughingly ask, 'How many camels you take?'

Fi was determined to see the real Tunisia. We were in Africa after all. The extent of her obsession was brought home to me. I was relieved when our two weeks were up and it was time to return home. We were going to try the new school and I was hopeful that I could get Fi back on track.

My efforts to get Fi back into school proved fruitless. Although the staff at her new school were very kind and did their best to reassure Fiona that bullying would not be tolerated, she was by now too worried that she would again become a target. She did attend for a few days, but I was soon to find out that she was slipping off to Elroy's flat. Then suddenly he disappeared. Fi found out afterwards that he was in prison.

It was during this time when Elroy was absent that Fiona met Zebbi, the pimp, for the first time, I don't know how or where. I do remember, very well, my first meeting with him. It was not auspicious. At the time he owned a blue Triumph sports car. One Saturday afternoon he drove up to Totley and knocked at our door.

He was small with long dreadlocks. There was a vague facial resemblance to Bob Marley. It's funny how instinct works. I instantly felt a strong dislike for him. He seemed very shifty and unable to look me in the eye.

'Is this a smoking house?' he asked me.

'I don't like people smoking inside,' I replied, 'but you can smoke in the garden.'

Rebecca was fascinated with his dreadlocks and asked if she could feel one of them. He complied and we all laughed.

What does a parent do in these circumstances? If I had known then that Zebbi, at twenty-six, already had convictions for theft and violence, I would not have let him into my house. If I had known that he was a regular drug-user, I would have shown him the door. My instinct to protect my children was always foremost in my mind, regardless of any compassion I might have felt for a fellow human being who had got himself into a mess. But how could I have known?

I was also trying very hard not to make racist assumptions. Even if I had suspected anything and had been unpleasant, Fiona would have accused me of being racist. So I sat tight and hoped that Zebbi was simply a colourful character who Fiona had brought home to meet us. I thought that if she was bringing people she mixed with home, I would at least know what was going on and be able to maintain some control.

The girls fussed over him, trying to stifle their giggles. He was like a celebrity to them. They made him coffee and a cheese sandwich. Then he asked me if he could take Fi for a ride in his car, promising to bring her back by nine. Although I was uneasy, I knew that if I refused I would push her into rebellion, so I agreed.

They went out for their drive and returned on time. Zebbi then asked me if he could take her to a 'gig' the following Friday.

'I'm a musician,' he told me, 'and I'm going to be performing. Fiona can stay backstage and I'll bring her back by two.'

'I'm sorry,' I said, 'but that's much too late. If I'd known you longer I might say OK, but I've only just met you, so this time it has to be no.'

'Oh, Mum, please let me go,' Fi wailed.

'She'll be all right with me,' Zebbi said. 'When I was a kid I used to go backstage with my family all the time.'

'She's only fourteen,' I reminded him firmly, 'and I'm not happy about it, so you'll have to accept it this time.'

He could sense that I was getting annoyed, so no more was said and he left.

I have a photo of Fiona at this time. If anything she looks younger than her age. She is also still wearing the fixed brace on her teeth. Then, I really couldn't think what attraction she could have held for Zebbi. I was so naive. Of course I know now. Men like him can spot their future potential earners at a glance. He marked her out then. He spotted her naivety and her vulnerability and he knew exactly how to get her, although he had to wait three years.

The following Friday, the day of the gig, I half expected some sort of protest from Fi, but none came. She seemed to have given up the idea – or so I thought. I was to be proved wrong.

At around nine that evening she slipped out of the house. I heard her go. Normally, if she was going out, she'd tell me where she was going and when she would be back. I ran down the drive after her, but she had disappeared. There was a queue at the bus stop, so I knew she hadn't taken the bus. For her to have vanished so quickly, someone must have been waiting for her in a car. I was annoyed but I had no alternative other than to sit back and wait for her to return.

The evening passed. John had gone away with his class at school. Rebecca was tired and went to bed. That was the first of many nights I was to spend waiting for Fi to come home. The minutes ticked slowly by. When midnight approached and she was still not back, I phoned the police.

There is a standard police procedure when a person is reported missing. Personal details are taken and a recent photo is requested. I gave a description of Fiona. She was 5 ft 4 in and very slim, about seven and a half stone. She had a fixed brace on her teeth. Her outstanding feature was her hair. She had a mass of thick, beautiful, dark brown curls, inherited from her Irish ancestors.

After the police had finished taking all the details, they left, telling me to try not to worry. 'She'll turn up in the morning, just you see.'

They told me they would check all the hospitals to make sure that she hadn't been admitted as a casualty. By now it was one in the morning.

I didn't even attempt to sleep. I was beginning to get worried. I had nothing to calm me. A strong drink would have helped, but I didn't dare in case I had to go out later in the car to pick her up. I sat by the telephone waiting for it to ring. I watched every bus arrive, willing her to be on it. I longed desperately to see her, head up in the air, hair flying, as she came down the road. When the last bus arrived at 2 a.m., and no Fiona, I was frantic.

Only another parent who has been through this can fully appreciate the fear and anguish. The imagination runs riot. I thought I might never see her alive again. If she was OK, why didn't she phone me? At three I rang the police to see if there was any news. They told me they had checked all the hospitals and she hadn't been admitted. Was this good news or bad?

They tried to reassure me. 'All our patrol cars have her description and they'll be looking out for her. She'll turn up in the morning.'

I spent the rest of that night pacing up and down, looking out of the window for her and willing the phone to ring. I watched the dawn break and morning appear. Still no Fiona.

When Rebecca woke up, I tried not to let her see how worried I was. She was only eleven. I was glad that John was away with his school and could escape some of the tension.

I phoned the police again: no news. I had told them

the previous night about Zebbi, and about my suspicions that she was with him.

'Have you found out where he lives?' I asked. 'I'm sure she'll be with him. He's no right to keep her away from her home. He knows she's only fourteen.'

'No, we haven't been able to locate him yet,' was the reply.

I decided I would have to do some looking myself. I fetched my mother over from her flat to man the phone. My poor mum. She was eighty-five. She was very close to Fi and terribly concerned to learn what had happened. She did her best to calm and support me. Rebecca came with me, and we set off to tour around town. For about an hour we trawled round the streets. We searched some of the grimmer areas of Sheffield, the dives and haunts of the criminal underworld, desperately hoping for a glimpse of Fi, but to no avail.

As we made our way home, I convinced myself that she'd be there waiting for me and my spirits rose at the thought. They were quickly dashed at the sight of my mother's glum face. There was still neither sight nor sound of Fiona.

I was beginning to feel really sick. My stomach was knotted. It was impossible to eat. All I could do was drink numerous cups of strong black coffee.

It was at this stage that I decided to do some detective work myself; the police were too slow for me. Zebbi had told me what his real name was and that his parents lived in a particular suburb bordering the city centre. I searched through the telephone directory and started phoning all the numbers with his surname in that area. I quite quickly located his home and spoke to his mother.

'My daughter is missing,' I told her. 'She's only fourteen and I think she might be with your son. Please can you tell me where he lives? I'm going out of my mind with worry.'

'Oh, my goodness,' she said, shocked. 'I'm so sorry. Is she really with Zebbi? This is dreadful. He hasn't lived at home for a long while and I'm afraid I don't know where he lives. I'm really sorry but I'm afraid I can't help you.'

It seemed strange to me, not knowing where your own son lived, but there was nothing more I could say to her, so I gave up on that line of enquiry.

I rang the police repeatedly during that Saturday. Each time there was no news. I couldn't concentrate on doing anything. Every time the phone rang, my heart leapt only to plummet back downwards when it wasn't Fiona.

Evening approached and still we waited. John phoned from his school trip and was full of the good time he was having. He was telling me about midnight feasts and badger watching in the grounds at night. I didn't tell him that his sister was missing. I was pleased he was enjoying himself. 'Be good and we'll see you tomorrow,' I said, hoping that by then Fi would be home and it would all seem like a bad dream.

I eventually persuaded my mum to go to bed. I knew I wouldn't sleep and prepared for my vigil by the phone. Rebecca, by now also dreadfully worried for her sister and upset at my anxiety, didn't want to leave me on my own. The second night was worse than the first. I couldn't help fearing the worst. I thought that Fiona must be lying dead somewhere. It was so out of character for her. She had no money with her. She hadn't even taken her coat. She was also such a home bird.

Why didn't she phone?

Rebecca and I sat cuddled on the sofa all night. She slept intermittently. Poor child. She was not unscathed by what happened to Fi. Even though they sometimes quarrelled ferociously, she always loved her big sister. Young as she was, she would often help Fi. At a time when Fi was scared to go upstairs on her own at night, Rebecca would always willingly accompany her. She was very indignant at the treatment meted out to Fi at school and was determined that the same would never happen to her.

The long night eventually passed and another day began.

I was racking my brains what to do when I suddenly remembered Zebbi telling me that he was a musician and that he had made some tapes. It dawned on me that the local recording studio might have some knowledge of his whereabouts. I quickly located the number and rang them. Sure enough, my hunch paid off. Luckily there was someone there, even though it was Sunday. They knew him, and when I explained what had happened, they immediately gave me his address.

It was so amazingly easy. Why hadn't I thought to do it before, and why on earth hadn't the police been able to find him? He lived in Lester Street in Pitsmoor. I am not sure how bad the area was then, but now it's a notorious area heavily involved in drug dealing and crime.

I phoned the police at once and gave them the address. They said they would call down to see Zebbi straight away. I felt a little relieved. I didn't think I could manage another night not knowing what had happened to Fi. My mum and Rebecca had some breakfast. I still couldn't eat and was surviving on black coffee.

A couple of hours later I phoned the police to see if there was any news.

'I'm sorry, but we haven't had time to check out the address yet,' the officer I spoke to said calmly. 'We'll get down there as soon as we can.'

I couldn't believe it. Was I going mad? How could they be so unconcerned? I knew *I* couldn't wait any longer. I was exhausted. I hadn't slept for two days, or eaten, and felt myself losing control and becoming irrational.

I phoned Fiona's father who was aware that she was missing and was as worried as I was. He came round immediately and we decided to go down to Zebbi's address ourselves. Rebecca was worried that something dreadful would happen to us, that we would disappear as well, so we decided she could come with us.

We set off in my ex-husband's car. Lester Street wasn't too hard to find, but we had a job locating Zebbi's flat. The street consisted of layers of dismal grey prison-like dwellings. I hope such a system of housing people will never again be considered by the planners. No lush green lawns or pleasant flowers for these inhabitants. This was the concrete ghetto, far removed from the semis with gardens in suburban Totley.

Eventually we spotted Zebbi's distinctive blue sports car and then found his flat. As we walked towards his door, I became anxious about my ex-husband.

'Whatever you do, don't hit him,' I said. 'It'll be you who ends up on a charge. Just stay calm.'

We knocked on the door – no answer. We knocked and banged a couple of times more. Still no reply. I lifted the letter box and, thank God, heard Fiona's voice.

I yelled through the opening: 'Open this door or the police will be down here.'

At that the door opened and Zebbi appeared. All he was wearing was a sparkling gold dressing gown. My anxiety of the previous two nights was replaced by a terrible surge of anger. I raised my hand and put all my strength into a stinging slap across his face. It resounded through the building. I was amazed at myself. So much for all my theories on non-violence. When the chips were down, I was no different from anyone else.

'You bastard,' I yelled at him, like the proverbial fish-wife. 'How could you abuse my hospitality like this? I welcomed you into my house. I trusted you and you took my daughter. You know she's only fourteen.'

'You've got it all wrong,' he said. 'She was wandering round the streets and I brought her here to be safe.'

'You're lying,' I shouted. 'The police were scouring the streets looking for her. They would've found her if that's what she was doing.'

At this point Fiona appeared. She was very subdued. 'I'm sorry, Mum,' was all she could say.

She told me that she had wanted to phone me but she hadn't any money and had been nowhere near a phone. 'I was coming home this afternoon,' she assured me.

She was still in the same clothes she had been wearing on Friday and she stank. She reeked of stale body odour. She had been smoking marijuana and, much later on, she admitted that Zebbi had had sex with her. He had apparently given her mangoes and cake in bed for breakfast afterwards.

This is how they operate, men like him. Initially they treat their women like princesses. Inevitably, as Fi was to learn, nothing comes free; in the end there is always a price to pay. But for Fiona, that time had not yet arrived.

My priority now was to get her home, but first we

had to go down to the police station to report that we had found her.

At Woodseats Police Station, the local station for our home, we were told that Fiona would be taken to the child abuse unit a couple of miles down the road. At this point Rebecca felt happy enough to leave us, so she was taken home to Granny by her dad. When my ex-husband arrived back, Fi was taken in to be questioned.

One of the officers at the door said to him, 'We're going to go all out to get him on this one' – meaning Zebbi. But we were very surprised, later, at what actually happened.

Then to our amazement, Fi refused to answer any questions. 'I don't have to answer and you can't make me be examined,' she told the officers. 'If you do make me have an examination, I can sue you for assault. Those are my rights and I know all about them.'

Zebbi had certainly tutored her well. I hadn't known this but apparently it is perfectly true. The Children Act of 1989 had given her the right at fourteen years of age to refuse a medical examination. In reality it had given her the freedom to choose to be taken advantage of by a man of twenty-six, a man already well known to the police and a regular drug-user. From conversations we had with the police at the time, I also believe that they suspected that he might be a pimp. In effect, in this instance the Children Act had taken away our rights as parents to protect our child and had presumed that, at only fourteen, my daughter would be able to recognise when she was at risk.

The police tried to persuade her to change her mind. They told us without her evidence or consent, they could do nothing. It was useless. Fiona remained loyal to Zebbi. I presume that he must have warned her that he would be in serious trouble if she told the truth.

They told her that men like him take young girls and force them to work the streets. 'He doesn't care about you,' she was told. 'He'll make you become a prostitute.'

Fiona wasn't listening. In her eyes, Zebbi could do no wrong.

I still find it very hard to take that the police know how these men operate, to the extent that they will warn young girls about them, yet they are powerless to stop their evil activities. If they suspected that Zebbi was a pimp, why could he not be stopped? Once again it seems to be the soft approach, the old sticking plaster remedies. We can't stop the bully, so we'll teach the victim to cope. We can't stop the drug dealers, so we'll 'educate' the children not to take drugs. We can't stop the pimps, so we'll warn the girls about them.

The sad thing is that many adolescent girls just will not be told. Pimps use a technique known as 'seductive grooming'. It is only too easy to trap a vulnerable and naive teenager in this way. In almost every instance the parent finds it impossible to compete, especially since the pimp is very rarely brought to justice. Fiona believed that the police were being racist in making these accusations against Zebbi, which made her even more determined to lie for him. Some youngsters, but they are few, manage to escape the clutches of the pimp. Others, like Fiona, pay the ultimate price.

I believe that men like Zebbi are evil. Time and time again, I ask myself, 'How can they get away with it?' Why, in this instance, did it all rest on Fiona herself to pin this man down? For God's sake, she was only a child, who should have been protected from such a man. I was told very definitely that unless Fiona made a complaint, the police were powerless to take any action whatsoever. If Zebbi could have been stopped at this stage, maybe I would have my daughter with me today.

The police did not give up on it straight away. They asked permission to question Fi on her own. They may have felt that she was being intimidated by the presence of her parents and that there was a chance she would speak more freely if we weren't there. So she was taken off and interviewed by a young policewoman. She told me later that she had had a grilling from this young woman. She said that she was given a cigarette first and then questioned. I was appalled at this as I knew that she didn't smoke then. It was as if a certain image of her had already been formed, far removed from what she was really like.

After this interview I was taken to one side and told

what Fi had said. Basically she had made up a story for them. She told them that she was not a virgin, and had lost her virginity, not to Zebbi, but to a boy in Tunisia. We were informed that no further action could be taken.

The police warned Fiona again about men like Zebbi, but they might as well have been speaking to the wall. Exhausted, we had to give up on it and return home.

As far as I am aware, Zebbi was never even spoken to.

My main emotion at the time was relief that Fi was safe. I didn't feel angry with her.

She was very subdued. 'I'm really sorry,' she kept saying. 'I don't want you to be so upset about me.'

I must have looked dreadful by this time. I had broken down and sobbed in front of her in the police station. She tried to reassure me that she could look after herself and that nothing was going to happen to her.

'Haven't you listened to what the police have been saying to you about men like Zebbi?' I asked her. 'I only go on like this because I love you and I don't want any-thing dreadful to happen to you.'

'When you go on and on like this I wish you *didn't* love me, Mum, if loving me means that you will try and stop me being with people who are nice to me,' she said in an exasperated tone of voice. And then, 'You've got to let me live my own life' – the eternal refrain of the teenager.

At this point I gave up. We were both exhausted. John

was expected home at any time. I ran her a deep hot bath and filled it with luxurious bubbles. She sank into it gratefully, after promising me that she would never stay away from home again without phoning me.

After this encounter, the relationship with Zebbi ended. It was not resumed until a few months before Fi was murdered. She did see him once down in Broomhall, the area where Elroy had his flat. She was in a phone box about to phone me. She told me that he had opened the door of the box and had screamed at her: 'Don't you ever bring your mother round looking for me again.' He had then struck her hard around the face.

In the meantime Elroy reappeared. It was a different-looking Elroy in that he had shaved off his locks in prison. I understand that Rastafarians are allowed to keep their locks, so I don't know why he was minus his. Maybe he was ashamed of himself. It is a sign of disgrace for Rastafarians to cut off their dreadlocks. Fiona was delighted to meet up with him again. I was none too pleased.

Although I hadn't been able to get Fiona to resume her schooling with the fresh start, I did not give up the hope that she would be able to continue her education.

The staff at her new school were very well-meaning, but of course they couldn't help Fi if she would not attend. Later on she told me that she used to get panic attacks at the sight of groups of teenage girls. Had she not become so fascinated with Rastafarianism, she might just, with the right sort of help, have been able to overcome her fears and get back into school. But it was not to be.

Her new teacher was Elroy. He had also had more than his own share of misery. Through him Fiona began to learn the basic principles of Rastafarianism.

Though I had guessed Fiona was still seeing Elroy, I was unaware of the extent of her involvement with him. After our meeting on that Sunday, I had told Fi not to see him. I had a pretty good idea that she was defying me and occasionally seeing him in town on a Saturday, but it was not until I realised she was not attending school that I became strongly suspicious that she was spending more time with him than I had thought. I had banned the relationship, so of course she didn't tell me. I was getting increasingly anxious about her.

After the episode with Zebbi, I began to wonder whether there was any truth in the tale she had told the police about having sex with a boy in Tunisia. It played on my mind. I kept thinking of a tale one of the travel reps had told us in the airport departure lounge as we left for home.

Apparently a girl had had a passionate holiday romance with a young Tunisian. As he waited to see her off at the airport, he gave her a small well-wrapped-up present, telling her not to open it until she arrived back in England. The girl imagined something precious, a token of their love, perhaps a ring. As the plane took off she was unable to contain her curiosity. With great anticipation, she ripped the wrapping off. To her horror, inside was a dead rat and, pinned to its body, the chilling message, 'Congratulations, you've just joined the AIDS club.'

The authenticity of this story was doubtful, but its moral was clear. It started to obsess me. Supposing Fi had had sex with one of the boys from the beach. What if she was HIV positive? In the end I had to know and spoke to her about it. Of course she couldn't back down on the story she had told at the police station, and so she agreed to come with me to the Hallamshire Hospital for an HIV test.

The first time we set off for the clinic, Fi said she felt unwell and would have to go home. The second time she went along protesting loudly. When we got there she asked if she could speak to one of the counsellors on her own. I waited outside. After about ten minutes, I was called in.

'Fiona didn't have sex in Tunisia,' I was told gently. 'There really isn't any reason for her to be tested.'

Despite feeling rather foolish, I was instantly relieved. We made our exit. What on earth must this woman have thought of us? At the time it really didn't matter to me. I was beyond caring.

I squashed the fear in my mind that Zebbi was probably more of an AIDS risk, and struggled to achieve some sort of rationality. At this stage Fi was still insisting that nothing had happened with him. I didn't believe her but it was only much later that she told me that he had seduced her. I had to live with my fears about AIDS. It soon became the least of my worries.

By now I was under a lot of strain. Rebecca and John were starting to grow up as well. My spare time was spent either writing up reports for work, or ferrying children back and forth.

One night Fi asked me if I knew where 'the square' was. The only square I could think of in Sheffield was Paradise Square, a well-heeled area in the centre, consisting mostly of solicitors' and estate agents' offices. I learned later that the square she was referring to was the notorious Havelock Square, later renamed Hanover Square to escape its reputation. This area was renowned at the time for drug dealing and prostitution. It was in this red light district that the 'Yorkshire Ripper', Peter Sutcliffe, was apprehended with a prostitute who was almost certainly saved from an untimely death by the intervention of the police. It was certainly not an area I would have had reason to visit. I was soon to become all too familiar with it. It was where Elroy had his flat and where Fi was starting to spend a great deal of her time.

Fiona's imagination was fired by Rastafarianism. It was one of the things which drew her to Elroy in the first place. The principles of this culture seem good to me. It is based on a peaceful and loving approach to life. It advocates living in harmony with the planet and accordingly many Rastafarians are vegetarians. Their god is Haile Selassie, the one-time Emperor of Ethiopia, referred to as 'Jah'. Western society, often referred to as 'Babylon', is seen as corrupt. The Oxford Dictionary defines a Rastafarian as 'a member of a Jamaican sect, regarding Blacks as a people chosen by God for salvation and having their true homeland in Africa'.

For the rest of her life Fiona had a dream of going to live in Ethiopia. There is a settlement of Rastafarians there who live off the land and are Rastafarians in the true sense of the word.

While I agreed with these fundamental principles,

there were many aspects of the culture which seemed very wrong to me. Always strongly opposed to any form of racism, I thought the suggestion that God selected people for salvation based on their skin colour racist in the extreme. I didn't like the open praise for marijuana and I was soon to find that most of the Rastafarians I met were using a variety of hard drugs as well, cocaine being the most popular. None of those I met were in paid employment and they all bore a tremendous grudge against white society.

'But they're not true Rastafarians, Mum,' Fi used to protest when I pointed this out to her.

'Well, let me meet a true one,' I used to reply.

'They can't live out their religion in this dreadful society,' she used to say.

'Well, they certainly know how to get what they want from it,' I would respond cynically. 'They don't seem to have any qualms about collecting their benefits.'

I tried very hard not to be racist. Perhaps it was just bad luck that nearly all the Rastafarians I met were heavily involved in the drugs trade. It is a great pity that these men have given their culture such a bad name.

I soon became aware that Fiona was developing more than a passing interest in drugs; which ones, I didn't know. On one occasion, I was tidying up her bedroom when I came across a small phial containing a powdered white substance. Unsure what it could be, but with a growing suspicion that it might be cocaine, I rang the local drugs project for advice. At the time I was totally ignorant about drugs. I would not have known what marijuana or any other drug looked like. A young man arranged for my substance to be analysed. The result, when it arrived, was perplexing: it was crushed and ground paracetamol. I was very puzzled, although obviously relieved. Was Fiona playing at drugs now? What was going on? I decided to tackle her about it.

She roared with laughter when she heard what I had done. 'I was only larking about, Mum. Honest.'

I also started to detect changes in Fi's behaviour and appearance. Always slim, she seemed to be losing a lot of weight. She often looked white and ill. I began searching her pockets regularly. I hated myself for doing this as I have always respected my children's right to privacy. This time, however, the stakes were too high. If my child was becoming involved with drugs, I had to know and I had to help her.

The first time I found cannabis resin in a matchbox in her pocket, I didn't know what it was. I phoned the drug centre and after I had described what I had found – a dark brown solid lump – they told me what it was. I threw it over the Co-op wall next to our house. After this, every time I found cannabis in Fi's pockets I threw it over the wall. I really didn't know what else to do with it.

Fi soon got wise to the fact that the stuff was disappearing from her pockets but she couldn't tackle me about it as that would have been admitting that she was

Irene Ivison

using it. She very quickly stopped leaving it about in her pockets, although I know that she continued to use it.

One Saturday I was taking John to a friend's house. Fi uncharacteristically didn't want to come with us for the drive. She usually loved to come out in the car; I would let her play her music on the car stereo, nearly always Bob Marley these days. Fi said she would stay at home. I could tell that she couldn't wait to get me out of the house. Some sixth sense made me go back and spy on her after we had said goodbye. Sure enough, there she was in the kitchen with a plastic pipe, made out of a lemonade bottle and a straw, preparing to smoke some substance, I'm not sure what. I was very angry with Fiona and seized the stuff out of her hand. For the first and only time she retaliated. She seized the nearest thing to hand, which just happened to be a chopping board, and caught me on the head with it. It certainly wasn't a hard blow. I didn't even feel it, but it must have landed on an area well supplied with blood, because suddenly blood started to gush down my face and into the sink. Fiona was horrified. She must have thought she had killed me. She ran to the phone and I heard her asking for an ambulance through her tears. I seized the phone from her, reassured the operator that I was OK and tried to calm her down. At this point poor little John came back in from the car where he had been waiting. Seeing my bloody face, he went white with fear. All three of us ended up cuddling together. It was an upsetting scene.

'This will have to stop,' I admonished Fi.

'I'm sorry, Mum. I love you. I didn't mean to hurt you. I'm really sorry,' was all she could say.

After this event I made it very clear that I would not tolerate illegal drugs in the house. I also started to educate myself on the use of marijuana.

'This damn drug,' I would rant.

Fi, of course, would have none of this. She was very well informed. But she was falling in love with Elroy. He would tell her all the good properties of marijuana, including its holiness.

I am sure that he was mentally affected by his very heavy habits. He seemed to be unable to function without drugs. All of his benefit money went on them and when this wasn't enough, he stole, even though he was ashamed of himself for doing so.

Gradually what was going on with Elroy sank in. Fi frequently didn't come in for her tea, and was often out in the evenings. Whereas before I had always known her friends, I had no idea who she was mixing with now. On one occasion she rang me in the evening and announced that she would be staying with a girlfriend overnight. I asked her for the address and the girl's name and reluctantly agreed that she could stay. I couldn't leave Rebecca and John, who were by now in bed, so I decided to check out the address in the morning. The next day I was not surprised to find out that the number of the house on the road which she had given me was non-existent. It was by now obvious that something was going on. I realised that Fiona's deception was due to the fact that she was doing something of which she knew I wouldn't approve. I could no longer trust her to tell me the truth and it hurt.

Because of this realisation I decided on a new tactic. I wanted to resume our previous open relationship. I felt it would be better for me to know what was going on even if I didn't like it.

'I won't stop you from seeing Elroy,' I told her, 'but you've got to agree to certain rules. You're definitely not to stay overnight with him in his flat. If you do I'll report him to the police. You're only fifteen and he's thirty-three. He's far too old for you.'

'Mum, I love him,' Fiona said. 'He's had a terrible life. I want to marry him and have his children. We're going to go back to Africa and live how we were meant to live. We've got to get away from this terrible society.' She was starry eyed as she spoke.

I understand now how fully she was indoctrinated by Rastafarian philosophy. I didn't at the time and I'm afraid I suggested rather unkindly that if this was what they really wanted to do, then Elroy should come off drugs, start to lead an honest life and look for a job. My words were falling on deaf ears.

We now entered a new phase. I was still hopeful that Fi would resume some studying. She was such a bright child. I had never had any difficulties with her as far as school work was concerned. She was one of those children who seemed to enjoy learning. All her school reports were excellent. To me it seemed such a waste of a fine brain.

I started to push the Education Authority to help us. It seems that there are no suitable placements for pupils like Fiona. There are units for non-attenders but they are filled with children who either have learning difficulties or have exhibited behaviour problems at school. They seem to be simply 'holding places' until the child leaves school with little hope of achieving any sort of educational qualification. I knew that Fiona would not fit into this sort of establishment. All the same I was desperate for anywhere which would keep her away from Elroy's flat and Broomhall.

In the event I was advised that attendance by Fiona at one of these units would be completely inappropriate. I was getting nowhere. There didn't seem to be any help for a child who was frightened to go to school because of her experience of bullying.

In desperation I went down to the education offices in town and more or less demanded to see someone in authority who could help me. An extremely kind person, who I believe was the Head of Special Education, listened sympathetically while I poured out everything that was happening to Fiona. The upshot of all this was that she was allocated six hours of home tuition a week to start straight away. I was grateful. It was the only option available and was obviously better than nothing at all. She would be able to do English and Maths GCSEs in this time and I hoped that when she was sixteen she would be able to pick up her education at one of the sixth form colleges.

In the meantime Fi's obsession with Rastafarianism was growing. One evening she phoned me and asked me if I could pick her up in town. I agreed and drove down to the meeting place. She was a little late in arriving and then I saw her bobbing along in the distance. She was animated and laughing. Fiona was one of those people for whom there are no shades of grey. She was either exuberant, enthusiastic and joyful or else dramatically miserable. On this occasion it was the former. She was accompanied by a good-looking young Rastafarian who was unfamiliar to me. She introduced him. He was known simply as 'B'. We chatted for a while and I remember mentioning to him that I would like to know more about the Rastafarian philosophy.

A few days later B phoned me at home. He asked me what it was that I wanted to know about the Rastafarians. I told him that I was worried about Fiona, who seemed to be becoming deeply embroiled in the subject. Because I was ill-informed, I was finding it difficult to form an opinion. B then invited me to meet him in town the next day for a chat.

I was very curious find out more so I went along. B

told me that he lived in a big old house in Pitsmoor and suggested that we go there for our chat. I agreed.

There was a large notice outside the house saying that it was dedicated to the furtherance of various religions and philosophies. We went inside and spent a couple of hours chatting over a cup of coffee. B was very well acquainted with his bible. I liked B very much and for once I was not given the impression of an angry young man seeking revenge on the white race.

I was still unhappy, though, with some aspects of Rastafarianism. I couldn't see that it was anything but wrong to suggest that black people were the only ones to be chosen by God for salvation. It is interesting to note that although its members would claim that Rastafarianism is a religion, it is not recognised as such in the UK. This is possibly because religious faiths should be open to all who adhere to their beliefs, not simply to those whose skin happens to be a certain colour.

I also found it impossible to identify Haile Selassie as God. He was certainly one of the first black men to give black people some dignity and status, and we can understand why he should be so admired, but this is not a good enough reason to regard him as God.

I was also rather unhappy about the status given to women. I never actually met any Rastafarian women, so I am not really qualified to make any statements on this with authority, but it appears to be a tradition among Rastafarian men to have many partners. Contraception is held to be wrong and unnatural, so one Rasta may have many female partners and numerous children. The woman of course is supposed to remain faithful and devote her life to keeping the man happy and rearing the children.

One might be moved to say rather cynically, 'So what's different?' The difference, of course, is that whereas women may well still be treated in this way in our culture, it would not be openly condoned or indeed even recommended. Rastafarian philosophy, rightly or wrongly, puts women firmly in their place, in the home.

I learned a lot from B. When I came to leave he presented me with a computerised picture he had done for me in the African colours of red, green and gold. 'IRENE. WHY OR WHAT DO YOU NEED TO KNOW ABOUT THE BLACK JEWS?' was its message.

For a while B visited us at home in Totley. The kids all liked him. He would come and play on the computer with them. We all enjoyed his company. I think Fiona saw him for a while but her main interest was Elroy and so we soon lost contact with B.

Our conversations at home seemed always to be centred around racism now. It appeared to me that Fi was being indoctrinated with a lot of anti-white propaganda. To my great sadness she started to become very upset because she wasn't black.

'We all originated from Africa,' she would say. 'Mum, I could say that I was African, couldn't I?'

I found this exasperating and often wondered whether she was completely sane. It didn't make sense to me how strongly she, a white girl, could be influenced by black, Rastafarian, philosophy. I have no difficulty understanding how this movement has become popular among young black people. We cannot deny the existence of racism towards black people and other ethnic minorities and this particular section of black society is hitting back. But I cannot agree that this is the way forward. To hit back at racism by becoming racist yourself can't be the answer.

Nowadays we often see and hear slogans such as 'Black is Beautiful' and 'Proud to be Black'. This is fine and I would certainly agree with them. The problem is that if a white person wore a T-shirt with 'Proud to be White', emblazoned all over it, they would be seen as racist. You can't have it both ways. A non-racist society would have no need to mention what colour a person is.

These are issues which our adult society has failed to resolve. It was not possible for my impressionable, sensitive and caring fifteen-year-old child to find her own way through this maze. I am afraid that we are a long, long way from Martin Luther King's famous dream.

Fiona used to cry over the slave trade. I have seen the tears pouring down her face. I also know that our many black friends have wept over what happened to Fiona. Maybe there is some hope in this simple truth.

One evening soon after the meeting with B, we were returning home in the car, having spent some time with family friends. Our route home bordered Broomhall. Fi was in the front of the car, Rebecca and John in the back. We were chatting casually when Fi suddenly became agitated and asked me to stop the car. Thinking that she felt unwell, I pulled over to the side of the road.

'Mum,' she said, 'I just have to nip down and see Elroy. I won't be long.'

'Oh no you're not, Fi,' I replied. 'You can't go wandering around there at this time of night. It's dangerous to be anywhere on your own and you know what it's like down there.'

'Mum, I'm sorry, but I've got to go and see him,' she answered. With that she jumped out of the car and ran off as fast as she could.

I was really angry and gave chase. Fiona lost her shoe but still she carried on. I eventually caught up with her on Park Lane. It just happened to be in a spot where prostitutes plied their trade. Two young girls were standing there.

'What's wrong?' they asked us.

Fi was crying and I was doubled over and out of breath.

When I told them that I was trying to get Fiona to come home with me, one of them said to her, 'Just look at me. I've been beaten black and blue in this game. I was sucked into it and I can't get out of it. I've got no other way to live now. You don't want to end up like me. Do as your mother says and go home with her.'

Fiona turned to me: 'Mum, I'm not going to be a prostitute. I'm just going down to see Elroy. I've got to tell him something. I promise I'll be back on the last bus.'

I had to let her go. I returned to the car and to Rebecca and John, their faces pinched and white with worry.

'It's OK,' I reassured them. 'Fi will be home later.'

True to her word, on that occasion she did return on the last bus.

However, very shortly afterwards, she started to stay out all night. The first time she did this, she rang to tell me that she was OK and that she'd see me in the morning.

'I'm stopping out, Mum,' was all she would say. Her speech sounded slurred and strange on the phone. She was also trying to speak with a Jamaican accent. I could tell that she'd been taking something. I couldn't get any sense out of her and when I tried to get her to tell me where she was, she hung up.

On this particular night my mother was staying with us, so I decided to go out and see if I could find her. I strongly suspected that she was with Elroy. I knew that he lived somewhere in Broomhall and set off down there in the car.

It was after midnight when I arrived in the area. I was a bit nervous but I was more anxious for Fi than for myself. There was a group of young black men with dreadlocks congregated around the chip shop as I pulled up near a block of flats. Fi had told me that Elroy lived in a flat, so I thought this would be a sensible place to start my search. As I got out of the car, I was suddenly aware that these young men were all running towards me, each racing to get to me first. It dawned on me that they thought that I must have come down there in search of drugs. I was right.

'D'ya wanna smoke?' I was asked.

'Draw? Coke? What ya wan? We can get it.'

I had to smother my rising hysteria. I couldn't believe they were openly selling drugs on the street. I found out later that this was a common occurrence. Almost every time I went down there I was offered drugs.

I told them that I wasn't interested in drugs but that I was trying to find my daughter. They were a friendly bunch. I asked them if they knew Elroy.

'This no place fo ya daughter, lady,' they warned me, but either they didn't know where Elroy lived or, if they did, they weren't telling me.

Then I heard a shout: 'Irene. What are you doing down here?'

It was Vernon, Fiona's friend from the Peace Gardens. To my relief, this was one of the rare occasions when he was actually sober. I told him I was looking for Fiona and he was very concerned.

'It's my fault,' he said. 'I introduced her to Elroy. She shouldn't be hanging around with him. He's far too old. She's only a child.'

Vernon always held himself responsible for Fiona. He often compared me to an African lioness. 'You are like the mother lion, Irene,' he would say. 'She fiercely protects her young from all dangers.'

But as we were to learn, even lionesses can't shield their young for ever.

'Come on,' Vernon said, this time. 'I can show you where Elroy lives.'

Together we walked to the nearby block of flats. We went up a couple of flights of stairs, past an old roll of carpet and other rubbish dumped in the stairwell and along a landing to Elroy's flat. His front door bore the imprint of a boot on the paintwork and looked as if it had been kicked in a couple of times.

We banged on the door but there was no reply. I shouted through the letter box, but if there was anyone at home they weren't going to answer. Vernon suggested we have a cup of coffee in his flat and try again later. We sat and chatted for a while and then returned to Elroy's. Again there was no reply. It was getting very late. I knew my mother would be getting anxious about me, so I decided I would have to give up the hunt.

When I got home I phoned the police and told them that my fifteen-year-old daughter had not returned home. They arrived at our house and took Fiona's details. I told them I had reason to believe that she was staying with Elroy, how old he was and that he did not have my permission for her to stay with him. They left, asking me to let them know when she returned.

I was not quite so anxious this time as Fiona had phoned me. I was concerned about her and worried about the marijuana I knew she must be smoking, and whether she was taking anything else. But mainly I was angry – very angry – with her for disobeying the ground rules we had laid down and with Elroy for taking advantage of her.

She came home in the morning, white-faced, exhausted and ill. I informed the police she was back. Once again she was given a good talking to by them when they called round to our house and to check that she was OK. So far as I know Elroy was not spoken to.

I really needed help by this time. I didn't know where to turn to or where to go to get it. In desperation I contacted the Social Services Department and asked to see a social worker. It was quite hard for me to accept that I needed help from the social services. I was a thoroughly middle-class woman with a professional job. I was more used to giving help than receiving it. I had never expected it to be so difficult to bring up my children safely. Now, with Fi, I was floundering.

People used to say to me, 'If my child was getting into drugs or disobeying me, I'd kill them.'

I'm sure I used to say the same thing myself. I know now that it is nearly always an impossible situation for a parent to deal with on their own. None of the disciplinary measures I had tried with her had worked. I had tried everything I could think of. I had dragged her, physically, back into the house when she was trying to go down there at night. I had gone to work with her trainers locked in the boot of my car. I stopped giving her her clothing allowance. Nothing worked.

I knew that, somehow, I had to make her see for herself that the path she was taking would only lead to further unhappiness. But as Fiona saw it, she had tried my way and been miserable. She was determined to look for some meaning to her life in another direction. I was powerless to stop her.

We were allocated a social worker who worked solely with young people. Her name was Christine. She did spend time talking with Fi. She would take her out for a cup of coffee and provide a sympathetic ear. I don't know whether or not she helped. She reinforced all the warnings that I was giving. I imagine that we were both saying exactly the same things. There was no change in Fi's behaviour.

One night when I went to pick Fiona up from Elroy's flat, I was really shocked at how unwell she looked. In the morning she told me that she had tried 'crack cocaine'. She had been drinking with a few other young people when some crack had been produced and passed around amongst them. Despite everything she had been told, despite Michael Jackson and all the education she had received about drugs, Fi had joined them.

'I didn't like it, Mum,' she told me. 'It made my mouth and nose sort of freeze, a kind of numb feeling, a bit like at the dentist.'

'Fiona,' I cried, 'you're a fool. How could you? What are you trying to do to yourself?'

'Mum, it was awful,' she said. 'They passed the pipe around. I'd no sooner had some than I desperately needed to have another turn. I'm not going to do it again, I promise you.'

'Where were you Fi?' I asked. 'Were you at Elroy's?'

'No, Mum, I wasn't. Elroy wasn't even there. He'd kill me if he knew. I went to his house later.'

She wouldn't tell me where this incident had happened. She knew I would have informed the police.

I know that she did have crack again and that she also took a variety of other drugs, morphine and methadone among them. I couldn't believe how easy it was for her to get hold of anything she wanted to try. What an unsafe society has been created for our young by the men of greed, the drug dealers and barons!

Although there was a lot of conflict between Fiona and me over this period, we remained very close. In our family we have always talked and discussed everything under the sun, regularly thrashing out topical issues over the dinner table.

Racism was by now the main, almost, it seemed, the only topic for discussion. We would debate this issue endlessly, Fiona always expounding Rastafarian views. She still had a history textbook from school and she would always leave this lying around open at a page showing a picture of Haile Selassie. One day it all got a bit too much for me. It was just after Fi had told me about taking crack. I was alone in the house and had just sat down with a cup of coffee and there on the table in front of me was the picture of Haile again, taunting me. In a rage I tore him out and ripped him up. Haile Selassie and Rastafarians weren't to blame but I was fed up to the back teeth with them all.

Fi laughed when I confessed what I had done. Some time later when the school asked Fi to return all her books, I owned up to my misdeed. They presumably thought that I was some sort of vandal and asked me for £7 to replace the book. I imagined them saying to each other, 'No wonder Fiona's got problems. Her mum's crackers.'

Next Fi decided to grow her hair into dreadlocks. There is apparently some biblical reference forbidding the use of a razor to the head, or so I was told. Rastafarians take this literally and never cut their hair. The derogatory term 'bald head' is used for someone who cuts their hair.

Fiona really wanted to be a Rastafarian, so she had to have dreadlocks. Fiona had the most beautiful hair. It was a mass of thick curls and I loved it. I suggested going to the hairdresser's and having her hair braided. This would not do. To get the hair to grow into locks it is necessary to stop washing it. Then as the hair grows it has to be persistently 'twiddled' until it forms the characteristic ringlets which are the dreadlocks.

Fi stopped washing her hair and started twiddling. There was a snag though. White people's hair is different from black people's. I have seen many white teenagers who have tried to achieve this hairstyle, beautiful in its own way, but without much success. Maybe like Fi they are not making a fashion statement, but do it because they believe in its religious significance.

After a few weeks of non-washing and twiddling, Fi's hair looked the most amazing mess. It was like a collection of rats' tails. To make it even worse, Elroy tried to help it along by putting some sort of wax on it, causing one big clump to stick together at the back of her head.

I tried really hard not to be embarrassed when we went out together but it was difficult to ignore the stares. She would usually tie it back in a ponytail when she came out with me so it didn't look quite so awful.

Round about this time Fi needed a new coat and so we went shopping together. She wanted a white mac in the trenchcoat style and we eventually found what she was looking for. She was exuberant, highly delighted with her purchase. Later, it dawned on me why she was so pleased. All the Rastas who stood peddling drugs on the street corners on 'the square' wore white macs. Fiona was living out yet another fantasy. This time it wasn't amusing. It was far too dangerous.

About four weeks after Fiona had first stayed out all night with Elroy, she did it again. This time she rang me up from a phone box at about 11 p.m. Her voice was slurred and I could hear a man laughing in the background.

'Mum, I'm staying out. I'm not coming home. I'm all right so don't worry.'

'Fi, who's that you're with?' I said, trying to sound calm. 'I want you to come home. Tell me where you are and I'll come and get you.'

I could hear more giggling from the man in the background.

'Fiona,' I screeched. 'You're not staying out anywhere unless you tell me where it is. I'll send the police down to Elroy's. I know where he lives now.'

'I'm not with Elroy, Mum,' she said. 'I'm going to stay with a girlfriend.'

'Tell me where, then,' I said, challenging her.

I could hear her whispering to the man in the background. She then gave me an address in Netherthorpe. It was in a block of flats, she told me, near the Children's Hospital. I asked her again to come home, but she hung up on me.

I was very worried and angry. I didn't believe she was staying with a girlfriend, but there was nothing I could do about it. Rebecca and John were in bed and I couldn't leave them to go and search for her.

The next day in my lunch hour I called at the address Fiona had given me. She had not been home when I left for work in the morning and I wanted to make sure that she was OK. A tall slim black man of about thirty opened the door. I recognised him at once as one of the white mac drug dealers who usually stood on the street corner. I tried to explain what I wanted. He shouted at me to come in. I was a bit frightened but as I had come this far I thought I might as well get on with it. I told him that I was looking for my daughter and that I had been given his address.

He was furious. 'Rasta blood clot!' he shouted. 'Wha yo think I am? Bloody white woman, I no got ya daughter.'

I thought he was going to hit me so I started backing towards the door. I was frightened. He was really mad.

He kept screaming at me. 'Rasta blood clot! Bloody white woman!'

I reached the door and ran to the car. I drove away from there as fast as I could. When I was far enough away, I had to stop the car. I was shaking. I cried hysterically for about ten minutes and then I pulled myself together and went back to work.

When I got home later on in the day, Fiona was in. I told her that I'd been to the address she had given me and how I'd had to run for it.

'Where were you last night, Fi?' I demanded. 'You weren't where you said you were going to be, and you could have got me killed.'

'Mum, I'm sorry,' she said, as usual. 'I was with Elroy. I love him. We'd been smoking ganja and when you asked where I was staying Elroy said the first address that he thought of. Why did you have to go down there?'

'I could have been badly beaten up,' I screamed at her. 'Don't you care at all?'

She tried to reassure me: 'Mum, I do care, but please don't keep running after me all the time. I will be all right.'

'I only do it because I love you,' I told her.

In exasperation, she replied, 'Don't love me so much then.' Then she looked at me and her tone softened. 'Mum, I'm not going to be here for long. I will never live to be old. I'm not happy here and I know that I will only be here for a short time.'

She had a faraway look in her eyes as she spoke. I couldn't get through to her.

'Don't talk like that, Fi,' I begged her.

I felt so afraid for her. Why did she keep saying that she was doing to die?

The next day in the car going to work, thoughts of Fiona's funeral kept coming uninvited into my mind. I could see the men carrying her coffin up the church aisle. Tears were rolling down my face and I was supporting my mother, John and Rebecca. I had to pull myself together and drive these thoughts out of my mind.

After this incident at the Netherthorpe flats, Fi never again made up a fictitious address. She did stay away from home a few times, but all she would say when she phoned was 'Mum, I'm staying out.'

I knew that she was with Elroy, and on every occasion I phoned the police and complained about him, but no action was ever taken to stop it.

I was by now at my wits' end. I didn't approve of Elroy or his way of life. Fiona was being exposed to a world of drugs and petty crime, which she was ill-equipped to deal with. She was only fifteen and she was in love. After her demoralising experiences at school she obviously found the heady experience of being liked wonderful. She was completely blind to the reality of the situation.

'Elroy is really nice, Mum,' she'd say to me time and time again.

'How can he be nice?' I would reply. 'He steals from

people. He takes what doesn't belong to him. That's not nice.'

'Well, we stole everything from his people. He can't get a job because he's black.'

'He can't get a job because he's dishonest,' was my reply.

We would have endless conversations in this vein, but I couldn't get through to her. I was quite shocked when once in conversation she referred to the police as 'pigs'.

I remonstrated with her: 'You may well find yourself wanting the help of the police one day.'

'But there's corruption in the police force,' she said. 'They pick on black people all the time. They often beat them up. They are racist.'

I tried to point out to her that the company she was keeping would certainly dislike the police: they had scant respect for the law as they spent most of their time breaking it.

A few weeks later Fiona again stayed out all night. A slurred voice came on the phone and simply stated, 'I'm staying out. I'll be home tomorrow.'

Yet again I phoned the police and complained that my fifteen-year-old daughter was being given drugs by this thirty-three-year-old man and that he was allowing her to stay with him knowing that it was against my wishes. All they ever seemed to do on these occasions was fill out the usual form. In the morning I would report that Fiona had returned home and they would call round, deliver a lecture to her and depart. On one of these occasions, one of the officers suggested that it might be useful for Fi to meet one of the community workers who worked specifically with young black people. I wasn't sure how this would help but decided to give it a go anyway.

It was arranged that this particular worker would visit us at home. One sunny morning I opened our door to Miriam Sulph. She was a very attractive and imposing black woman in her mid thirties. She was accompanied by a smaller, older black woman wearing a smart blue hat, whose name was Mary. They came in and we had tea and biscuits and talked. They were trying very hard to help the young black people in their community to steer clear of trouble. Miriam had raised three sons by herself on the Kelvin Estate, another notorious housing block, recently demolished.

'They've been brought up in the middle of all this trouble,' she told me, 'and they've had to learn how to keep themselves out of it.'

Mary lived in Pitsmoor. She too was worried about the drug dealing, blues parties and crime on her doorstep.

When Fiona mentioned some of the Rastafarians she had met, both women shrieked and threw up their hands in horror.

'Zebbi,' Miriam told her, 'is a cokehead. I remember seeing him lying on the floor in one of the toilets at a club. He was crying and screaming for sugar water. Stay away from him, Fiona. He'll have you on the streets working for him.'

'I'm not having anything to do with him,' Fi assured them. 'I'm going to marry Elroy.'

They didn't actually know Elroy but told Fiona that he was much too old for her. They invited us to a party which was being held down at the police station, telling Fi that young black and white teenagers would be mixing there and that she'd enjoy it. We chatted for a while longer and then they left.

I was very grateful to these women for trying to help us. We did actually attend the party but the young people there were more Rebecca's age. I liked Miriam and so did Fi. She bumped into Fi on a few more occasions and they would always be pleased to see each other. Once we saw her in the bank shortly after Elroy had given Fi an engagement ring.

'Look, there's Miss Sulph, Mum,' Fiona said. 'I'm going to tell her that I'm engaged to Elroy.'

She bounced up to Miriam full of her news. If Miriam was surprised she never showed it.

That autumn – 1991 – I tried to persuade Fi to register at one of the sixth form colleges to do some GCSEs. Unfortunately the Home Tuition had been abandoned after about 2 months. Fiona had been slipping away to visit Elroy instead of waiting at home for her teacher so we were not able to continue with these sessions. At fifteen she was still a year too young but in the circumstances they accepted her.

When it came to filling out the registration form, she wanted to put down 'black' as her ethnic origin.

'All mankind originated from Africa,' she insisted, 'so it will be all right for me to put that down.'

'You're going to look pretty silly when you turn up at college then,' I replied, exasperated and by now heartily sick of the whole issue of colour.

In the end she saw sense, but she didn't want to say she was English and so she put down 'Irish' as her nationality. At least it was nearer the truth. I was sad that the company Fiona was keeping had made her feel so ashamed of her nationality.

'You aren't to blame for past mistakes,' I would say to her time and time again. 'You weren't even there. We have to go forwards.'

But it was useless. She did start some GCSE courses at college, including one on African Culture, but she dropped out after a few months.

Up until this time Fiona had only seen Elroy at his flat. He had not been to our house in Totley. One day I got home early from work and spotted Elroy crossing the road to the bus stop, accompanied by Fiona who was clearly upset and looked as if she had been crying. I went into the house and started to prepare tea. I was angry with Fiona for bringing him to our house and was preparing myself for a confrontation with her. Then a sudden thought struck me. I had rather foolishly hidden £60, three weeks' child benefit money, in a drawer in one of the bedrooms. I had saved it to buy a present and provide a party for John's eleventh birthday. I went upstairs to check and my suspicions were confirmed: the money was gone. No wonder Fiona was looking so upset. I sat on the floor and started to cry.

Just then Fi came back in. She didn't attempt to deny what he had done. She looked very ashamed.

'I'll make him give it back, Mum, I promise.'

'He'd better give it back to me by tomorrow or I'm getting the police,' I said.

I was very surprised indeed when Elroy did return my money. Fi said that when she told him it was for

John's birthday he was ashamed and gave it back to her.

Once, when Rebecca had stayed away from school with tonsillitis and I called home to check on her, I discovered that Elroy had again been in the house and they'd been smoking marijuana there. I was really angry.

'He is not to come to our house,' I shouted at Fiona. 'You are not to bring him here.'

I felt really at a loss as to what to do for the best. If Elroy didn't come to our house, then Fi would go down to him at Broomhall. In the end I decided that our home just had to be a drug- and crime-free area, or we would all sink. I had to think of Rebecca and John as well; they were becoming increasingly affected by events. So I stuck to my guns and Elroy remained banned from the house.

The next time Fiona phoned to say she was staying overnight with Elroy, I took a further step: I warned her that I was going to insist that the police come down with me to his flat. When she didn't return on the last bus, I phoned them and demanded that someone should come and help me bring my daughter home. I was appalled that in all this time, so far as I knew they had never even spoken to Elroy.

'Please will somebody meet me outside this man's flat and tell him he is not to encourage my daughter to stay with him,' I said, begging this time. 'I thought this sort of thing was against the law.'

They agreed for a police car to meet me at the flats, where an officer would speak to Elroy.

I drove down to Broomhall and waited. It wasn't long before a young officer arrived. He accompanied me up to the flat. We were just in time to see Fiona at the door and Elroy walking away. She looked terrible. Her face was ashen and she was unsteady. Her voice was slurred as she spoke and she tried to assume a Jamaican accent, speaking in patois. I could tell that she had taken something.

'Fuck ya, pig. I no wan go home,' she shouted.

I was ashamed. I couldn't believe that this was my child speaking. This was the first time I had ever heard her using language like this. The word 'fuck' was forbidden in my house and I would have been very angry if any of the children had used it, even though it seems commonplace now.

The policeman then went up to Elroy and said, 'Look here, mate. You do know that this girl is under age, don't you?'

Elroy shrugged his shoulders and muttered, 'I'm not stopping her from going home.'

And that was it. The officer helped me to bundle a loudly protesting Fiona into my car, shouting at her, 'Do as you're told.'

We set off towards home with the police car following us. We'd gone a few hundred yards when Fi started to kick up a tremendous fuss in the car. Still using patois, she yelled, 'Let mi out, I wan go back to Elroy's.'

She started to open the car door as the car was moving. I was forced to slow down.

'Shut the door, Fiona,' I screamed, leaning across her to pull it to.

She opened it again, oblivious to any danger in her stupefied state. The police car behind us flashed me to stop.

'You're never going to get home like this. You'll have to leave your car and come with me.' He warned Fiona that if she misbehaved in his car, he would arrest her and she would spend the night in the cells.

When we arrived home I was distraught, Fiona was white-faced and upset but still strange and defiant.

My mother, who'd been waiting at home, took one look at us and said to me, 'You poor thing.'

Her sympathy was too much for me and I broke down and sobbed. I begged Fiona to stop behaving in this way. By now she was quieter.

'I'm sorry, Mum,' she said.

Later on we all went to bed and I tried to sleep. At some point in the early morning I heard Fiona slip out of the back door. I was too exhausted to go after her again. I was beginning to feel defeated.

The next morning I went down to the social services office in town. I asked to see somebody, anybody who could help me.

'I'm at my wits' end,' I sobbed.

I was taken into a quiet room to talk to a young social worker. I was in a terrible state and although I tried hard to control myself I couldn't stop crying.

'I just can't understand it,' I told her. 'I had understood that it was illegal for a man to have sex with a girl under the age of sixteen. Here is this man who is thirty-three with a criminal record, giving my fifteen-year-old daughter drugs and letting her stay overnight with him. The police know about it, Fiona's social worker knows and nothing can be done because Fiona won't complain. Of course she won't complain. She thinks he's wonderful because he's kind to her. But she's only a child. She's meeting all sorts of people who I'm worried are going to have a bad influence on her down there. She's so impressionable and she hasn't got a lot of common sense. Why can't something be done? Why do we have these laws? They're useless.'

I carried on like this for a while. She listened, nodding her head sympathetically, but she wasn't able to offer me anything other than the chance to come down and get it off my chest. She said she could stay in touch and visit me from time to time if that would help. I accepted her offer and in the event I did see her a couple of times, until she became pregnant, when the contact stopped. To be perfectly honest, I wanted more than just someone to talk to. I wanted Elroy to be stopped. I wanted Fiona away from Rastafarianism and sanity restored to my home.

I was beginning to understand why people took the law into their own hands. The next time Fiona phoned me to tell me she was stopping out, I phoned the police as usual and then the social services. I was put through to the duty social worker. I told him what was happening. He was very sympathetic but once again told me that nothing could be done.

'If it was my daughter,' he said, 'I'd go down with my brothers to Elroy's house and we'd give him a beating. It's the only language men like him understand.'

The next day I went down to Elroy's flat and scratched 'PAEDOPHILE' in big letters on the tiles surrounding his front door. Then I knocked on the door.

When he opened it I attacked him. I hit him and punched him with my fists, crying and screaming, 'Leave my family alone.'

Fiona appeared from behind him and yelled at him, 'Don't hit my mum.'

Elroy merely grabbed hold of my shoulders while I jumped up and down like a puppet trying to hurt him. It was futile. I might as well have been hitting a rock. I eventually crumpled into a sobbing heap.

'Look,' Elroy said. 'Fiona wants to stay with me. If she didn't stay she'd be wandering around the streets.'

'No, she wouldn't,' I replied. 'She'd come home. All you've got to do is tell her that you can be friends but she's got to wait until she's older before she can stay with you. What you're doing is against the law. You're not to give her drugs either.'

I knew I was wasting my time. He had scant respect for the law – and hadn't he told me when I first met him that marijuana was so beneficial I should bake it into cakes and give it to my children?

Fiona came home with me and I tried to talk to her rationally. Then she casually informed me that she wanted to have Elroy's child. She had this wonderfully rosy view of living as a family with Elroy and their children.

'But you couldn't support a family. You haven't got any money and any that you do get he will spend on drugs,' I warned her.

We discussed contraception. I suggested she should go on the pill.

'But Mum, I couldn't do that,' she exclaimed. 'Contraception is wrong. It's a white man's trick to stop the black race from multiplying.'

I laughed out loud. 'Don't be so damned stupid. You must use something. If you and Elroy have a child it will be put on the Child Protection Register straight away.'

It was useless. I just could not compete with the influence Elroy exerted over her.

The next time I saw Christine Johnson, Fiona's social worker, I mentioned this conversation and my very real fear that Fiona would become pregnant. She too was appalled.

'I'll have a word with Fiona and see if she'll come with me down to the family planning centre.'

Fi did go down to the centre. She refused the pill and an injection of Depo Provera, but came home with a bag of condoms. Later I found her having a great time in the bathroom with Rebecca and John, making water bombs with them.

The whole situation was ridiculous. Here was my young daughter in an illegal and what I considered an abusive relationship. Her social worker knew what was going on but the only help which could be offered was advice about contraception. It was pointless anyway. Elroy had told her that he had a fourteen-year-old son he never saw. She felt that if she gave him a child it would hold him to her. He had also convinced her that contraception was unnatural. She started to long for a baby. She was still only fifteen.

For some reason Fiona failed to conceive. This may well have been a result of the drugs she was taking. Elroy still insisted that the 'holy herb' could do no harm, even to an unborn child.

Then Fi confided in me her fears that she might be infertile. 'Elroy's going to go to the doctors to see if it's his fault. But it can't be, can it, because he's already got a child?' she said. 'It must be me.'

'Fiona, you're not old enough to have a baby,' I said. 'Your body isn't mature and you're also abusing it with drugs.'

I was horrified that Elroy was going to go to his doctor to see if there was a problem with his fertility.

'Has he told his doctor how old you are?' I asked.

'He hasn't been yet, Mum,' she said.

'This is ridiculous,' I ranted. 'Fiona, you can't be so

stupid and irresponsible. You can't bring into the world a child you're not able to look after.'

As usual, my words were falling on deaf ears.

The more I thought about it, the more anxious and angry I became. The situation was farcical. I could see Elroy being put on some course of infertility treatment in order to be able to impregnate my teenage daughter. Nothing would surprise me any more.

It niggled at me so much that I decided to ring the doctor's practice in Broomhall which I presume Elroy attended.

'I know you're going to think this is a rather strange request,' I said to the receptionist who answered the phone, 'but I'm so concerned I've got to do something.' I then explained the situation to her.

She did her best to reassure me. 'I'll make a note of all this and have a word with one of the doctors. I obviously can't discuss another patient's treatment with you, but I will pass this information on.'

I had to let it rest at that. Fiona, to her great disappointment, never conceived. I sometimes wonder whether a child might have made a difference to her. It might have given her a focus in a life which was, at that time, pretty aimless. Maybe it would have saved her. On the other hand it might not have made any difference and we would have been left to bring up a poor motherless child while trying to explain the tragic circumstances leading to its mother's death.

Around this time I was so desperate that I began to consider leaving Sheffield. It wouldn't have been easy. I had a good job, I owned my own house and John and Rebecca were settled at school. I also had a lot of very good friends in Sheffield. Whenever I brought up the subject Fiona used to say that she wouldn't come with us.

With hindsight, how I wish I had followed my instincts. I often hear now of families who have moved away from large cities to places like Cornwall or the Hebrides, with the specific purpose of rearing their children away from the perils of today's large cities. I doubt that Fiona would have stayed behind on her own. She was always close to us. Even after our worst arguments, she would throw her arms around me and tell me that she loved me.

She made me a card for Christmas that year. 'Mum, you're great,' it says.

My mother would always say, 'No matter how awful

Fi is, you can't help but love her.'

It was so true. Her endearing characteristics made you very quickly forget her bad behaviour. She was always very thoughtful and loved to give us little gifts she had made. I have many of these tokens to remember her with.

In the autumn of that year, Fi decided that her dreadlocks weren't quite right and, to my relief, she decided they would have to go. Before she could change her mind I asked her where she would like to have her hair done.

'I'll pay for you to have whatever you want,' I promised.

'I can't have it cut, Mum,' she reminded me. 'Rastafarians never have their hair cut. Can I go to Chez John and ask him what would be the best thing to do?'

'OK,' I agreed.

Chez John was an Afro-Caribbean hairdresser's on the edge of the city centre. He was amused and horrified when he saw Fi's hair.

'Please can you get it out without cutting it?' she asked.

'I'll do my very best,' he assured her.

John and two of the other hairdressers took turns trying to comb out the knotted raggedy mess of Fi's dreadlocks. 'It's going to be a long job,' he warned me, so I took a walk around town.

When I returned I could tell that Fi was close to tears.

Two hours of tugging and pulling at her hair was obviously taking its toll.

'I'm afraid that we're not going to be able to comb this big clump out,' John explained, indicating a particularly large knot of hair. 'We're going to have to cut it if you want it out.'

'I can't have it cut,' Fi protested.

My heart sank. 'You've got no choice,' I said.

Finally defeated, she agreed to the scissors, to the hairdresser's and my great relief. Her hair was cut to shoulder length and a beautiful young woman emerged. Even though she'd had to break her principles, Fi was pleased. When, a few weeks later, the fixed brace was removed from her teeth, the transformation was complete. The girl who had come bottom of the list the boys had made at school was turning into a highly desirable young woman.

The loss of her dreadlocks, though, did not signal any diminution in Fi's obsession with Elroy and Rastafarianism. She told me again about the land in Ethiopia which 'Jah' had given to his true followers.

'One day, Mum, Elroy and me are going to go there. These people aren't corrupted by greedy white man's society. They live off the land and they grow all their own food.'

'Do they smoke draw then?' I asked.

She smiled. 'Yes they do, but they grow it themselves. They smoke it when they have prayer festivals. Mum, please will you try it? You've got no idea how clearly it helps you to see things. It's really wonderful. It makes you feel so good. If everybody used it there'd be no fighting or wars. People would be happy.'

She genuinely believed that one day she would go and join the Rastafarians in Ethiopia. It was her dream, far removed from the lives of many of the dealers she knew of in Sheffield. These men, their bodies bedecked with gold jewellery, rode around in their BMWs, enjoying a rich lifestyle on the profits they made from the drugs trade and from their exploitation of young girls in prostitution.

One evening I was very surprised, and alarmed, to receive a phone call from Elroy.

'Where's Fiona?' I screeched. 'What have you done with her?'

'She's not very well,' he told me. 'Can you come down and pick her up?'

'Why? What's wrong?' I asked him suspiciously.

'She's all right,' he said, 'but she wants you to come and get her.'

It was quite early in the evening. My mum had been spending the day with us so she agreed to stay on with John and Rebecca while I went down to Broomhall.

They must have been looking out for me because as I arrived they were walking down the stairs from Elroy's flat. He had his arm around Fiona's shoulders. I remember this well as it was the first time I had ever seen him make any outward display of affection towards her. As they got nearer, I could see that her nose was swollen and both her eyes were ringed in black.

'My God, what have you done to her?' I cried.

'It wasn't Elroy, Mum,' Fiona explained quickly. 'It was Yvonne, a girl who lives around here. She's been saying that I'm stuck up and that I've been talking about her. I was on my own in the flat. Elroy had gone out for some draw. She knocked on the door. She was with some of her friends and when I opened the door she laid into me. Mum, I wasn't talking about her, honest.'

Elroy shrugged his shoulders and joined in. 'I told Fiona not to open the door to anyone when I'm not here, and I also warned her what that Yvonne's like. She won't take no notice of me though.'

For once I sympathised with him.

'Please can you take me home, Mum?' Fiona said. 'My nose kills and I've got a headache.'

She said goodbye to Elroy and got into the car.

'Fi, I think you ought to have your nose checked out at the hospital. It looks as if it might be broken to me,' I said.

She agreed, so we went to the casualty department at the Children's Hospital. She was X-rayed when we arrived and, as I'd thought, her nose was broken. We were told that with luck there wouldn't be any disfigurement, but they couldn't do anything until the swelling went down anyway. In the event, Fi was left with a small bump on the bridge of her nose, a permanent reminder of her life down in Broomhall.

'You know, Fi,' I said in the car on the way back, 'we really should report this girl to the police. She's a bully and she shouldn't be allowed to get away with this sort of thing.'

'Mum, if I complain, she'll make my life hell. She'll come after me and beat me up again. I know she will. I wouldn't be able to go and see Elroy again and you won't let him come home, so I can't do anything about it.'

We had to leave it at that. I wasn't going to change my mind and let Elroy come to our home. I had Rebecca and John to think about. So do the bullies of this world continue. In my heart I was hoping that this episode might make Fiona spend less time at Elroy's flat and more time at home with us.

Shortly afterwards, I saw Christine Johnson, the social worker, again. She told me she had an idea which might help: under the Children Act, a case conference can be arranged to discuss any problems relating to a child, when it is felt that the child might be in danger.

'We've got nothing to lose,' she said.

I agreed, and for the first time felt that something might be done to stop Elroy. I asked Christine to go ahead with the arrangements, and to make sure that I would be allowed to be present. I knew from personal experience how some professionals work, and I was determined that my views as Fiona's mother should be taken seriously.

Fiona's life at this time wasn't all conflict, though. Down at the square she met a young woman, Sandra, who became a firm friend. I think Sandra was about twenty when they met. She lived with a young Rasta, Ben, and they had two adorable children, Joseph and Sophie. Ben looked up to Elroy and told me that Elroy was a very wise man. He had assumed the role of guru to Ben.

Fi told me later that the two men would use one of the downstairs rooms in Sandra's flat as their own private blues den. 'They play their music really loud and get completely off their heads.'

Fiona was often included in these sessions, much to Ben's dismay. 'He's jealous of me and Elroy,' she would joke.

Sandra's children loved Fiona and Elroy. She often helped Sandra to look after them. She often told me little things they had done: 'Joseph called Elroy a "Biscuit tramp" today, Mum, because he was eating all the biscuits.'

Sometimes Sandra and Fi would go out and enjoy themselves, giggling together, just two girls having fun. They were very close.

Sandra was often shocked at Fi's outrageous

approach to life. 'Oh Fiona,' she would shriek, 'you're a hopeless case.'

One day Sandra phoned me at home. She sounded very worried. 'It's Elroy,' she told me. 'I've seen him with some crack cocaine. I really didn't think he was into hard drugs. If he gets Fiona on to that stuff, she's had it. I honestly thought he only ever smoked draw.'

I was worried too. 'Did you ask him what he was doing with it? Does Fiona know he's got it?'

'I did ask Fiona about it,' she said, 'and she told me that he'd found it. I really am worried about Fiona. She's so young. I had thought that Elroy would look after her, but now I'm not so sure.'

'I'll have to think about what to do,' I told her and thanked her for phoning me.

When Fiona came home in the evening I told her what Sandra had said.

'No, Mum,' she said, laughing. 'Elroy's not on crack. He found it. They raided CJ's club last night. All the men in there threw all the drugs that they had over the wall into the yard. Elroy found the rock in a plastic bag this morning.'

CJ's was an illegal blues club on the square. Periodically the police would raid it, close it down and take the owners to court. They usually found large amounts of illegal drugs and, on one occasion I read about in the paper, machetes and other weapons. The owners would be fined and the club would be open again for business within a few weeks of the raid.

'Well, what's he doing with it then?' I asked.

'I don't know, Mum,' she answered, 'but I think it's worth a lot of money. He says he's going to throw it away, though.'

A likely story, I thought.

'I'm not happy about this, Fi,' I said. 'It's highly addictive. Have you had some again?'

'No, Mum, I promise. I haven't and I won't.'

For the time being I had to leave it at that, although I was terribly worried. I saw Sandra a few days afterwards and she indicated to me that she wanted a quiet word.

While Fiona was amusing the children, she whispered to me, 'My dad says that he can help you. Meet him in the Botanical Gardens tomorrow morning at ten-thirty.'

I nodded and said I would go along.

I couldn't believe how my life was changing. How on earth had I got mixed up in all this? All I wanted, yearned for, was an ordinary life, being happy with my children, and now here I was, going to a secret assignment with a man who had, as Sandra openly admitted, been involved in some unsavoury dealings.

'I love my dad, though,' she'd told me, 'and his heart's in the right place.'

A few years before, I wouldn't have considered meeting him, but I was totally disillusioned with the proper channels. No matter how often I complained to the social services and the police, no action was ever taken against Elroy. They seemed to think that because Fiona went to him willingly, then it was OK.

I had been told that the case conference would take place the next week, and I did hope for some result from this. Nevertheless, I was interested to hear what John, Sandra's father, had to offer, so the next morning I drove down to the Botanical Gardens as arranged.

It was one of those bright sunny early winter mornings. I met John, a small, good-looking, roguish man, by the old bear pit. The stern features of Queen Victoria looked down on us from her statue as we sat on a park bench and chatted.

'Do you know what's going on between Fiona and Elroy?' he asked me.

'Yes, I do,' I said, 'and I'm very angry about it, but I can't do anything.'

'He's addicted to smoking draw,' he said. 'That's all he thinks about. He is crazy. He shouldn't be with your daughter. She's far too young.'

'Don't I know it.' I sighed. 'But I can't get her away from him.'

'Did Sandra tell you he's on to crack then?'

I told him what I knew and about all my efforts to stop the relationship.

'I can help you,' John said. 'I can make sure that he disappears and isn't seen for a very long time.'

He must have noticed my worried expression then

because he tried to reassure me. 'He wouldn't be hurt. He just wouldn't be around and Fiona would be safe away from him.'

'But what would you do?' I asked.

'I can't tell you,' he said. 'But I promise you, it would work. You must be really worried about Fiona.'

I couldn't believe this was happening to me. 'I presume that you wouldn't be doing this for nothing. How much would it cost me?'

'Well,' he replied, 'I could do it for £200.'

He waited for my reaction. I had suspected from the start that he was going to say something like this. Even so, when he actually did, it took my breath away. I knew there was no way I could even consider what he was suggesting.

'Thank you for your help,' I told him, 'but I couldn't be involved in anything like that. I'm going to push the police further. There must be something they can do.'

He laughed derisively. 'You're wasting your time. They daren't do anything because he's black. If it had been a white man of his age having a relationship with an under-age girl, giving her drugs an' all, he'd be locked up by now. I tell you, girl, if you're going to get your kid out of this mess, you got to do more than complain to the police. They won't do nothing about it.'

'I'm sorry,' I said, 'but there's no way I could do what you're saying.'

He shook his head sadly. 'I tell you now, it won't stop. Don't say I haven't warned you.'

With that our conversation was finished. John walked back with me to the gates of the gardens. All the way home I thought about what he had said. Were the police really afraid of being accused of being racist? Surely not. It niggled away at me for a long time. But even if I had thought this was true, I couldn't possibly resort to John's vigilante approach. I still couldn't come to terms with how people like John lived. It seemed they saw themselves as outside the law. They had their own rules and they asked no one else to protect them. It wasn't for me then or now.

The case conference took place the next week on a dismal wet November afternoon. I parked outside the social services department building, Redvers House. After a few minutes, I was shown into a small room. Already present were two members of the police child abuse unit and four social workers, one of whom was Christine Johnson, Fiona's allocated worker. There was an apology from the Child Protection Office.

In my work I had attended many conferences called to plan the welfare of a child, so unlike many parents in this position I was not in awe of the proceedings. I had written out a rough summary of events which I gave to each member of the panel. It follows here:

Report for Case Conference – Fiona Ivison d.o.b. 5.2.76
18.11.91

My daughter has been associating with Elroy Bishop – age 33 yrs for approximately 1 yr. During that time Elroy Bishop has:-

1. repeatedly supplied her with marijuana – I do not know whether he has given her any other drugs.
2. had and continues to have an unlawful sexual relationship with her. My daughter has told me this is so and Elroy Bishop has admitted it to me.
3. refused to use contraception – contraception being a white man's ploy to stop the black population from increasing and it is against Rastafarian principles. Rastafarianism is a religion which he claims to believe in.
4. harboured her in his flat when she should be in school – indoctrinated her with all sorts of Rastafarian anti-white beliefs.

I have reported this to the police on many occasions and have been told that nothing can be done due to difficulties in proving any of the above. My daughter is besotted with this man and cannot be persuaded to see sense at the moment. Elroy Bishop has also repeatedly been to my house even though I have told him he is not welcome and have forbidden him to come. On one occasion I arrived home to find him smoking marijuana in my lounge. He has stolen money from me – £60 – which Fiona eventually made him return and only last week when I arrived home he was again in my house eating my food – my twelve year old daughter Rebecca was also in – not being at school that day because of illness. In short I feel persecuted by what this man has done to my family and am not prepared to put up with it any longer. I am now very worried again as Fiona has told me that Elroy had 'found' some crack – three rocks – in a plastic bag following a raid in CJs. She told me that he threw it away but I do not believe this. I have today reported this to West Bar Police Station [14.11.91]. Unfortunately none of the drug squad officers were there but I am told this will be investigated.

My concerns must be obvious to everybody. The effect this last year has had on my family will remain with all of us. My 11 yr old son and 12 yr old daughter have had to live in a desperately upset family situation and have been exposed to the dangers of the drugs scene. I know that Fiona has sought this man out and has willingly gone to his flat. However she is extremely naive and most normal men of 33 yrs of age would not have treated a 15 yr old girl in this way.

I have obvious concerns about the future for Fiona. I am also concerned about my two other children who are increasingly upset by our family problem. I am extremely angry that nothing can be done to stop Elroy

Bishop from abusing my daughter Fiona in this way and am asking this panel for help.

Irene Ivison (parent of Fiona)

We discussed the problems at length.

'I can't understand it,' I said, struggling to keep calm. 'We all know what's going on here. The police know, Christine knows. This man is giving my daughter drugs. He's having sex with her and won't even use contraception. For God's sake, he's thirty-three, he's got a criminal record. My daughter is fifteen. Why can't anything be done about this situation?'

'Mrs Ivison, we do sympathise,' was the answer, 'but we can't do anything unless we can prove what's going on.'

'But the police have brought her back from his home in the morning. She's told me and she's told Christine what's happening. She's a child, for God's sake. Christine has even been down to the family planning place with her to try and persuade her to use contraception,' I wailed.

With a sickening feeling, I realised that I was not going to get an answer this time either. The young police officer on the panel volunteered to go down and warn Elroy that what he was doing was wrong. This young man was supportive and told me that I could contact him in the future when problems arose.

I was told that it was up to me whether I wished to insist on legal intervention by the department. They decided that as Fiona was obviously from a good, caring background, there would be no purpose in putting her name on the Child Protection Register. That was the end of the conference.

Once again I began to feel I must be going mad. Of course she wasn't in any danger from me. Perhaps these conferences were only supposed to be about children who were being abused by their families. I thought that if a member of Fiona's family was doing to her what Elroy was, there would be no question of leaving it up to me to take legal action.

I had had genuine hopes of this conference. I was left disappointed and disillusioned by the outcome.

A fortnight later I received a copy of the summary of this meeting, included here.

STRICTLY CONFIDENTIAL

RE: FIONA IVISON (DOB: 05.02.76)
CASE CONFERENCE HELD AT REDVERS HOUSE, FLOOR 6,
18TH NOVEMBER 1991 – 4.15 P.M. TO 5.15 P.M.

Present: Mrs A Wilson, Acting Principal Social
            Worker Division 3 (Chair)

Mr P Devlin, Principal Social Worker Division 3

Ms C Johnson, Social Worker Division 3

Mrs I Ivison, Fiona's mother

Ms I Todd, Court Social Worker Family and Community Services Department

PC J Skekton, Sexual Offences/Child Abuse Unit – Heeley

DCM Froggatt, Sexual Offences/Child Abuse Unit – Heeley

Apologies: Hilary Owen, Child Protection Office

This case conference was convened by Christine Johnson under the Child Protection procedures and Chaired by Ann Wilson. In the absence of a Minute taker the following are notes of the recommendations which followed the discussion of Fiona's circumstances.

1. DC Froggatt agreed to liaise with South Yorkshire Police Drugs' Squad because of concerns about Fiona's exposure to drugs and drug taking at the home of Elroy Bishop.
2. DC Froggatt also agreed to visit Elroy Bishop to reinforce the concerns about his relationship with Fiona Ivison.
3. Christine Johnson undertook to continue to work with Fiona in the hope that she would begin to

recognise the risks to which she was exposed because of her relationship with Mr Bishop.

4. It was agreed that there would be no purpose in referring Fiona's name to the Child Protection Register at this stage.

5. It was further decided that legal action by the Department would be unlikely to be productive.

It was acknowledged following these recommendations that it was open to Mrs Ivison to reconsider whether she wished to insist on legal intervention by the department and that that would have to be responded to appropriately if and when it arose. There was no decision at this stage about reviewing the situation formally in a case conference but it would clearly be open to any of the participants to reconvene the case conference if that seemed to be necessary.

Paddy Devlin,
Principal Social Worker (Division 3)
                    D3/PD/JMG/29 November 1991

The only other option open to me was to place Fiona into care. If I had thought that this would keep her safe, I would have had no hesitation in doing so. However, time and time again, I was warned by the police and social services: 'Don't put her into care. She'll be far worse. They can't keep an eye on them and she'll get into all sorts of bad company. She'll be ruined completely if she's in a children's home.'

I was appalled then as I am now by this admission. What sort of a society have we become when our children aren't even safe 'in care'? How can we send children who may have been suffering badly in their own homes into an environment where they, on the social services' own admission, are likely to be even more at risk?

Although I considered taking legal action, I never did. I had scant faith in the system and I didn't have enough money to seek legal advice. Because I worked, I knew I wouldn't be eligible for legal aid.

Much later, in March 1992, when Fiona was sixteen and the relationship was legal, I wrote to the Chief Superintendent of South Yorkshire, expressing my dismay at the inability of the law to protect girls like Fiona. His answer was sympathetic but suggested no way forward and is included here.

SOUTH YORKSHIRE POLICE

DIVISIONAL HEADQUARTERS
50 WINDSOR ROAD
SHEFFIELD S8 8UB
TELEPHONE (0742) 500700

ALL COMMUNICATIONS SHOULD BE ADDRESSED TO "THE CHIEF SUPERINTENDENT"

Mrs I Ivison

Your Ref:
Our Ref: E/JSG/AA
DATE: 29 APRIL 1992

Dear Mrs Ivison,

Thank you for your appealing letter of 30 March with which I have much sympathy and understanding. However, it does appear that you have been well briefed and you are aware of the inadequacies of policy, the law or Agencies to assist you in your difficult circumstances.

Your comments have been passed on to the officers in the case. Thank you for taking the time to write to me.

Yours sincerely

J S Gough
A/Chief Superintendent

Fiona was sixteen in February 1992. I asked her what she would like to do on her birthday and she said she would like us all to go out for a meal together. She asked if Elroy could join us but didn't press me when I said no.

It was a good day. We all sang 'Happy Birthday' to Fi and gave her presents. In the evening we went to an Italian restaurant – a happy family occasion. I looked at my three beautiful children and thought, 'Why can't we always be like this?'

I hold that memory like a cameo in my mind. It was a temporary lull in Fi's stormy life, and for a short while we recaptured some of the serenity we had known as a family.

Now she had reached the legal age of consent. I was becoming resigned to the situation; I recognised my powerlessness. She remained as infatuated as ever with Elroy.

'I want to marry him,' she declared. 'Now I'm sixteen we would be allowed to get married if you gave your consent.'

'No way, Fi,' I told her. 'In years to come you'd turn round and blame me for letting you do it. Wait until you're eighteen and then, if you still want to, you can go ahead without my permission.'

In her heart she knew I would never give my consent.

'Mum?' she said. 'Who'll pay for my wedding? I'd really love a long white wedding dress.' Then she mused, 'Where would I get married, though? There's a High

Church of Ethiopia. Do you think I could get married there?'

It was a nice dream. I went along with it for her sake. I was sick of arguing with her.

'We don't know what we'll be doing in two years' time,' I said. 'You'll just have to wait and see.'

We didn't know then that two years later, on her eighteenth birthday, there would be no wedding flowers for her, just red roses on her grave and a congregation of shocked and grieving people.

I was more or less resigned to the situation, because I couldn't do anything to change it. I certainly wasn't happy about it. I really did not like either the way Elroy lived or some of the people Fiona was meeting in his company. I was increasingly concerned at the number of young addicts she knew. Whereas I was shocked to the core when she told me how some of these people lived, Fi seemed to accept it as a normal way of life. She even knew casually a girl who worked as a prostitute.

I don't believe Elroy was a pimp. Fi told me she could never be a prostitute.

'I've met some of them, Mum,' she told me. 'There's one who lives in the next block of flats. She's had a terrible life. She now injects heroin and everybody says she's gone mad.'

She pointed this woman out to me once. She was only a girl. My heart went out to her.

'Fiona,' I said, 'promise me that you won't end up

like her. You wouldn't do that for anyone, would you?'

'Mum,' she said, 'Elroy's not a pimp.'

'Are you sure?'

'The nearest he's ever done to something like that,' she told me innocently, 'was when he was in London. He stood outside this house where he knew a prostitute was doing business, and he told this man who came along that he was taking the money for her. The man gave him £20. Elroy pointed him up to the prostitute's room and when the man was out of sight up the stairs, Elroy ran off as fast as he could.'

She laughed at this tale. A few years back I would have been horrified, but I had been learning a lot. Most of it I would have preferred not to know.

I was appalled at the world Fiona was exposed to. Many of the young people she met were involved in drugs, crime and violence. I found it so hard to believe that she could want to associate with them. She would always have an excuse for them, and indeed many of them had led horrific lives; in many ways they were victims themselves. Those she stayed friends with always showed kindness towards her and I know that they looked after her down there. But it was really only Elroy that she wanted and loved. She saw something special in him and, at that stage, I honestly believe she would have died for him.

All the same, I still wanted her away from there, even though she'd told me that she would be miserable without him. I wanted her at home with her family and away from this twilight world she was so ill-equipped to deal with. Time and time again we discussed the dangers of her lifestyle, as the warnings of the police, particularly in relation to drugs and prostitution, echoed in my ears. Although she assured me repeatedly that she could keep herself safe, I was not convinced.

We discussed prostitution continually.

'I could never do that, Mum,' she told me. 'I tell you what: I bet you £20 that I'll never be a prostitute.'

Twenty pounds was a lot of money to Fi then.

'OK,' I said, 'if you're still mixing with the company you're keeping now when you're twenty-one, and you haven't become a prostitute, I promise I'll give you £20.'

This conversation was in a light-hearted vein. I never for one moment thought that this was a bet that she was destined to lose.

Not long after her birthday Fi began to talk about leaving home.

'Mum,' she said in an excited voice, 'I could get a flat. If you go to the council and tell them you're homeless, they'll give you somewhere to live.'

'Where on earth have you heard that?' I said. 'Anyway, you're not homeless. You've got a good home.'

'Mum, it's true,' she replied. 'All you've got to do is sign a form saying that you can't have me living at home and they'll give me a flat. Oh please, Mum, please do it.

Elroy's flat is so awful and damp. If I had a flat I could do it up really nicely, and he could come and see me there. I could get away from Broomhall so you wouldn't have to be so worried about me.'

'I couldn't do that Fi,' I said.

She didn't press further this time, but she was soon nagging away at the subject again. 'I can't see why you won't help me to move out,' she'd say. 'Don't you want me to be happy?'

She went on about this so much that I decided to check out if what she was saying was correct, and it was. All that was needed was for a parent to sign a form saying that they were no longer going to provide a home for their youngster and the council would house that child, as long as he or she was at least sixteen. I have since heard of many young people, with perfectly good homes, who have been given accommodation in this way. I was told that the youngster would have to live in a hostel for a while, but it usually wasn't too long before a flat was allocated. Because they know this is possible, many young people will make their parents' lives intolerable until they wearily give in.

Fiona was very determined. A flat of her own where she could do as she pleased without my constant nagging seemed an ideal solution to her. 'Please sign the form. You won't really be throwing me out. We both know that. I'd come and see you every day, I promise.'

Then she warned me that if I didn't do it, she'd be

forced to behave so badly that I would be really pleased to see her go. 'Mum, I really don't want to upset you any more,' she pleaded.

How I cursed Sheffield City Council.

If there had only been Fiona to think about, I would never have given in. But for the last two years our family had been badly upset by her exploits. The endless arguments about her relationship with Elroy and my increasing anxieties over her connections with the world of drugs had taken their toll. Rebecca and John were getting very upset by the unhappy atmosphere in our house. Rebecca would not sleep easily at night unless I assured her that I wouldn't be going down to Broomhall. I had often had to take her with me late at night to bring Fi home. I felt very guilty at taking a child of her age down into a red light area late at night, but I had little choice. John was not so affected. Once asleep, it would take a bomb to wake him up. I used to leave a note for him on these occasions, 'Gone to get Fi', in case he woke up, but he never did.

Mainly because of my fears for Rebecca and John, I eventually agreed to what Fi was asking. It was not done easily and I felt heartbroken when the form arrived for me to sign.

Fiona was allocated a room in a hostel, quite near the centre of town. She did all the arranging and negotiating herself; I refused to help her. On the day she moved, she had packed her clothes, along with Robert and

Fringe, and was ready to get the bus down there when I relented and said I would give her a lift. Rebecca came with us. I tried so hard not to cry. I tried to think of all sorts of other things to take my mind off what was happening, but I could not stop the tears from rolling down my face.

'Don't cry, Mum,' Fiona begged. 'I'll be all right. I really will. I'll phone you every day, I promise.'

I was unable to speak. We dropped her off at the hostel and Rebecca and I held hands all the way home in the car. By the end of the evening I started to feel a little better. Maybe this was what Fiona needed to do to find out that living away from home was not the rosy little dream that she expected.

Fi kept her word and either phoned or visited us at home every day. After about two weeks, she confessed that she wasn't enjoying life at the hostel and that she would have to wait about ten weeks to get a flat in the area that she wanted.

'I've decided that I'm going to move in with Elroy,' she told me.

I was not altogether surprised. I wasn't happy about it, but once again I knew there was nothing I could do. If she couldn't be stopped when the relationship was unlawful, there was no chance at all of intervention now that Fiona was sixteen.

I told myself that maybe this would be the quickest way for Fiona to get it out of her system. Let her live down there, let her see what it's really like without the comforts of home to run to every night, let her stand on her own two feet, I thought, and she would either survive it or come home, a far wiser young person. And maybe, just maybe, one who had learned some important lessons about life.

Elroy's flat was in a pretty dreadful state. I am not sure how long he had been living there when Fi moved in, but he certainly hadn't done anything to make it into a comfortable home. The flat consisted of a living area with cooking facilities, one bedroom, a bathroom and a separate toilet. The whole ceiling in the living room was stained a murky yellow, a relic of the previous occupant's taste for curry, I was told. The bedroom had mould in the fitted cupboards and all along the window sills. Elroy never used it, so it was never heated and the damp grew much worse over time. The floors were uncarpeted and the walls were covered in ancient peeling wallpaper. Furniture was sparse. There was a table and some chairs, a TV and an old sofa bed, which Elroy slept on. Most other possessions, the cooker and a stereo, for example, were temporary. They would appear for a while and then he would sell them to pay for marijuana.

Once I had accepted that Fi was going to live down

here, I visited her in the flat from time to time. When I was there, Elroy would usually either go out or hide from me in the bedroom. I didn't understand how she could put up with such conditions. She was a very fastidious person. She always looked clean and smart herself, even when obviously under the influence of drugs.

I would drop massive hints about cleaning the flat, such as 'Why don't you get some bleach and a scrubbing brush at that mould in the bedroom?'

I itched to clean it up myself, but although I did eventually buy them a big bottle of bleach, I refused, on principle, to do it for them, and so the bedroom remained abandoned to its fungal condition.

After some weeks, Fiona managed to persuade Elroy to do some decorating. He painted the curry ceiling and she chose some pretty wallpaper which they put up in the living area. I gave her some old curtains and they acquired a piece of carpet. Robert and Fringe, who'd moved in with her, assumed pride of place on an old dresser which appeared from somewhere.

Although I could never forgive Elroy, I had to accept the situation. In his own way and to the best of his ability, he did look after Fiona while she lived with him. He never treated her like a skivvy – God help him if he had. He washed his own clothes and hers too at times. He often cooked for both of them. Fi told me that he observed the Rastafarian practice of not letting a menstruating woman perform any domestic tasks. So once a month, it seemed, she was given a rest from domesticity. I don't know what the reasoning behind this was, but it seemed like a pretty good idea to me.

Elroy, like Fiona, was a committed vegetarian. He introduced her to various Jamaican dishes such as sweet dumplings, rice 'n' peas and sweet potatoes. Apparently his sweet dumplings were out of this world. He would make a big plateful and they would dip them into a bowl of sugar as they ate them. It was probably just as well that Fi was never one to put on weight; she would have become huge on Elroy's dumplings in no time.

Fiona had no money of her own. I flatly refused to give her any. There was no way I was going to finance this relationship. She had chosen of her own free will to live away from home and I was determined that she would have to stand on her own two feet. I did, of course, help her in many other ways. I didn't want to lose contact with her and I wanted to make sure that she knew that her home was always with Rebecca, John and me.

They applied to the DSS and Elroy's benefit money was increased to allow for Fiona living with him. Fi was cross that this extra money was given to Elroy and not to her. I think she was worried he would spend it all on drugs. She herself was always an excellent manager of her finances, a trait certainly not inherited from me. I had to admire the way she budgeted. I don't know how she did it but she managed to persuade Elroy to hand money over to her every week for their living expenses. Every Saturday I would pick her up at the flat and take her to Morrisons for our separate weekly shop. Usually we had a coffee and a chat in the café too, where I would buy her a large cheese and pickle sandwich, as she was often hungry.

I haven't been to Morrisons since she died. I can't bear to go there. Maybe one day, when I can, I will know I am starting to get better.

Now that she was living with him, Fi was beginning to realise that Elroy's behaviour was sometimes rather odd.

'Mum,' she told me once. 'I went shopping with Elroy during the week and he was really strange. He wouldn't buy anything unless it began with the letter C.'

'What did you buy then?' I asked.

'Well, we bought crisps, coffee and chocolate.' She laughed.

'Fi, he's mad. For goodness sake. A man of his age doesn't *do* things like that. Why don't you come back home?'

But she wasn't ready to leave him yet. I was having serious doubts about his sanity. I felt sure that the large amount of marijuana he used had seriously damaged his brain. I had chatted to him a few times and I noticed a difference from when I had first met him. Then I had found him intelligent and interesting. Now he often rambled when he spoke, sometimes completely losing the thread of a conversation.

He also had some unusual ideas and theories. Fiona told me about a conversation they had had about vegetarianism. He placed a cup, representing God, a saltpot, representing animals, and a pepperpot, representing man, on the table.

'God came first,' he said, moving the cup to the head of the line, 'and then the animals and then man. Why then should man turn around and eat the animals?'

I think he thought he was being quite profound, but Fiona often used to giggle about this. Later, as his behaviour grew more bizarre, she would be embarrassed by him.

Some things about him, Fiona found childlike and endearing. He once made a drink which consisted of hot chocolate, coffee and ten spoons of sugar. He called the concoction '10cc' and made up an advert for it which he would sing with an exaggerated American accent. It made Fi laugh. I imagine he was pleased to amuse her.

Sometimes he would sit with pen and paper and write certain words down, 'marshal' and 'children', for example. He would then sit and stare at these words for long periods as if they were a source of wonderful inspiration for him.

Clothes sometimes posed difficulties for him. For a long time he decided to wear only corduroy trousers because 'corduroy goes with my name, Elroy'. He also became obsessed with owning a suit and eventually obtained one from a catalogue. He wore it continuously for three weeks and then got rid of it.

'Where's your suit?' Fi asked him when he appeared without it.

'I had to get rid of it,' he told her. 'It was becoming evil.'

The same fate befell a mirror they had. Elroy became convinced it had very evil properties and wasn't happy until Fi had thrown it away.

When people say that marijuana is harmless, I often think of Elroy. Admittedly he used it to excess, but I am sure that his brain was affected by it. I had read up quite a lot by now on the side effects of marijuana and I could see what was happening to him. I was interested to learn that the incidence of paranoid schizophrenia is considerably raised among heavy users of this drug. To my dismay I realised that Fiona was also using it heavily. I was upset when she told me that she was starting to have panic attacks and severe palpitations. She told me that the marijuana helped her to relax and calm down. To her it was still the wonderful 'holy herb'.

Quite soon after she moved in with Elroy, Fiona found a job as a waitress in an all-night café in the centre of town. She worked there for a couple of nights a week, for which she was paid the princely sum of £1.50 an hour. This café, Porkys, is now closed down. At the time Fi worked there it was a thriving business, catering for the needs of the nightclubbers as they staggered out, hungry yet not wanting to go home, at two in the morning.

Fi used to finish work regularly at 4 a.m. Elroy never let her walk home on her own, even though Porkys was only a short distance from his flat. He would walk down to the café, wait for her to finish work and then see her back to the flat.

She told me that he had been really entertaining one evening. He had been drinking and when he turned up at the café he was in high spirits.

'Oh Mum,' she enthused, 'you should have seen Elroy last night. He was dancing in Porkys. It was ever so good. He actually did a backwards somersault. All the customers stopped and watched, and when he sat down, they all gave him a big round of applause.'

She was delighted that Elroy had been respected and liked by the late-night revellers.

On another occasion, Elroy wasn't so amenable. Fiona was by now an extremely attractive young woman and she was beginning to realise it. She never forgot her ugly duckling days when she came bottom of the list of girls who the boys in her class would most like to kiss.

On the evening in question, on her own admission, she had been flirting with one of the young waiters at Porkys. Elroy was waiting to walk her home and she hadn't realised that he was watching her and getting really angry. To Fi, it was simply light-hearted fooling around, but Elroy felt she was making him look small. All of a sudden, he had had enough. He walked over to the sink where Fiona was washing some dishes and landed her a vicious blow. Her right eyebrow was split and blood poured from the wound. Elroy ran from the café, chased by one of the waiters, but years of running had made him a good athlete. Fiona was very shaken but refused to go to hospital. I'm not sure what happened later on that night, but I suppose they must have made up the quarrel as she was with him at the flat when I called around the next day.

That morning, I knocked on the door, prepared for the usual wait. The door was never opened straight away, presumably because too many people were looking for Elroy. Normally his hand would appear at the letter box, pushing it open so he could see who was outside, before he opened the door. When he saw it was me, he would usually call Fiona and let me in. On this particular occasion, the hand that pushed the letter box open was small and white, and the eye that appeared was bruised and swollen, black and blue. She opened the door and I saw the full picture.

'Who has done that to you, Fi?' I screamed.

She looked shamefaced. 'Mum, it was Elroy, but it's all right. I deserved it.'

'For God's sake, where is he?'

I pushed past her and into the bedroom where I knew Elroy would be hiding. I shouted and screamed at him for what seemed like ages. Fi tried to silence me a few times, but there was no stopping my furious outpouring.

'So this is what men like you do,' I taunted. 'You hit and beat young girls? Aren't you brave? What chance does Fiona have against you, eh? You can't get your own way unless you beat her into submission, is that right?'

I didn't give him a chance to reply and I didn't want to hear anything he had to say. He never answered me back. He could quite easily have silenced me in the same way he had treated Fiona, but he sat there in a corner of the room with his head down. It was as if he was saying, 'I know I was wrong. I deserve this.'

Afterwards I thought back to what Fiona had told me about Elroy's own childhood. He barely knew his own mother. Maybe things would have been different for him if he had had a better start. His mother had died when he was very young. When he was fourteen his father had collapsed and died in front of him. The young Elroy was sent to live with relatives. He was not happy with them. As a young man he had escaped this situation and set up home with a girl he loved passionately. They had a son and for a while they were happy together. Then the young woman met another man. She left Elroy, taking his son with her. He was apparently broken by this experience. He left Wolverhampton, where they had been living, and came to Sheffield. Fi once met some friends of his who had known him at the time. They told her that he had never been the same after his girlfriend had left, taking his son. They thought he had suffered a breakdown, and blamed his unhappy past for his present situation.

I hoped that after this incident Fiona might start to realise what her life was going to be like if she stayed with Elroy. But she told me that he had promised not to hit her again.

'I love Elroy, Mum,' she told me. 'I never want to leave him.'

I know he did hit her again, but never as severely. Later on she told me about an occasion when he had lost his temper and she had called the police. Elroy was warned about his behaviour. Fiona didn't want to press charges. She just wanted him to know that she would get him into trouble if he persisted in being violent towards her.

'He hasn't hit me since, Mum,' she told me.

I wasn't convinced. I hoped fervently that she'd soon see sense and return to the safety of her own home.

Life was never tranquil for Fiona down at Broomhall. One morning Elroy went out, locking her in the flat. He said he wasn't going to be long, but when he hadn't returned by mid afternoon, Fi was getting a bit fed up. One of her friends called round and Fi told her through the letter box that she couldn't get out. Between them they decided that the best thing would be to phone the fire brigade. The only way out of the flat was through a window two floors up. To her great embarrassment, Fi was carried down a ladder over a fireman's shoulder. There was applause and much good-natured cheering from the other firemen as they witnessed Fi's rescue.

'It was really funny, Mum.' She laughed as she told me.

I wasn't that amused. 'Why does he lock you in when he goes out?' I asked.

She made up some excuse for him, but the next time I saw her she waved a key triumphantly. 'I'm OK now, Mum. Elroy's got me my own key.'

I supposed it was progress of a kind.

Fi did visit us at home frequently during the year she lived with Elroy. I didn't realise at the time quite how hard it was for Rebecca and John. One of the things which sometimes happens when you have a child who is 'going off the rails' is that the rest of the community seems to close around itself, in order to prevent its children from going the same way. It is very easy for the siblings of the wayward one to find themselves outcasts.

Fiona had certainly committed a great social sin in Totley by associating with a black Rastafarian. Rumours about her drug taking were rife. It seemed to me that Rebecca and John were now being tarred with the same brush by certain members of the community. I say this without bitterness. I fully understand any parents' desire to protect their children from people who are involved in drugs. But when people are frightened for their children, humanity often takes a back seat, and innocent kids suffer the repercussions.

One afternoon Rebecca went to call on a boy she had befriended. They were both thirteen. When the boy's mother opened the door and saw her, she shouted, 'Clear off. We don't want no druggies round here.'

Rebecca was very upset and angry and she admitted to me that she was very rude to this woman. This incident hurt and shocked both of us.

Sometimes on summer evenings, Fiona would join Rebecca and her friends in the local park. There was one particular twelve-year-old boy who repeatedly asked Fiona to sell him some marijuana. She always refused, but one day she got sick of this childish pestering and gave him a small stone, telling him it was cannabis resin. It was a joke, really. I heard them laughing about this youngster getting stoned on a stone. Later on I learned that the mother of one of this boy's friends had earlier heard the youngster boasting that he could buy 'draw' from Fiona. This parent had turned detective and asked the boy to buy some for her, thinking that Fi would then be exposed as a drug dealer. I'm not sure what her reaction was when he turned up innocently with the stone.

This parent's behaviour was very upsetting. To my

knowledge, Fiona never sold drugs; I'm quite sure she wouldn't have given them to children.

There was another episode, when Fi had been spending the evening with us and had gone with Rebecca to the local youth club. Apparently Elroy joined them for a short while. I got a telephone call at home from Woodseats Police Station.

'Would you come down and pick Fiona up please,' said the voice on the other end. 'We arrested her on suspicion of selling drugs.'

'What?' I yelled. 'Oh no, she wasn't. I don't believe it. I really don't.'

The police officer spoke calmly. 'It's OK. We couldn't find anything on her, and there's no evidence that she was doing anything like that. Someone rang us and told us that Fiona was at the youth club with her Rastafarian boyfriend. They told us that they'd heard she was selling drugs, so we had to check it out.'

'Well, was she?' I demanded.

'No, she wasn't,' was the answer. 'But because she's still a juvenile and we arrested her, we have to make sure you, as her parent, understand what happened.'

'I'm on my way,' I told them.

When I got to the police station, Fiona was grinning widely from ear to ear, and joking with the police.

She laughed when she saw me. 'I've been wrongfully arrested. I should be able to sue them for false imprisonment.'

'This isn't funny, Fi,' I said. 'We have to live in Totley. For God's sake, don't bring Elroy up here again.

I wished that those parents who were so vigilant against Fiona had turned their energies to the real drug dealers. If I had caught Fiona selling drugs, I would have had no hesitation in handing her over to the police myself. Fiona was a victim and with her my whole family.

One Saturday when I called to take Fi to Morrisons, she came running down the stairs, beaming all over her face.

'Mum, Elroy's bought me a ring. Look.' She flashed her engagement ring finger proudly under my nose.

It was a nice little ring, with a small sapphire surrounded with cubic zirconia.

'Oh come on, Fi,' I said wearily. 'Where did he get this from? It's stolen, isn't it?'

'It's not, Mum. Honestly it's not. He saved the money out of his giro. I went to choose it with him. I can show you the receipt.

My scepticism could not dampen her joy and enthusiasm.

Later on that summer of 1992, she told me that they had made marriage vows to each other. They had devised their own ceremony, a mixture of African lore and biblical prayers. How she loved him. She told me then that even if she wasn't always with him, a part of her would always love Elroy.

In the autumn of that year she once again raised eyebrows in Totley by bringing Elroy to the annual barbecue at her old school. After her death one of her friends told the local newspaper about this event, saying that Fiona had done it because she liked to shock people. You have it wrong, my friend. Fiona did what she did because that was how she was. I don't think she ever deliberately set out to shock anybody. They came to the barbecue together because she loved him and wanted him with her.

Christmas approached, bringing a dilemma for Fiona. I still refused to allow Elroy into the house because of his stealing and drug taking. She begged me to let him come and join our family Christmas.

'He'll be all on his own, Mum,' she pleaded. 'He's never had a proper happy Christmas like we have at home. Couldn't he come, just this once? I promise I won't ask for him to be allowed here again afterwards. It would be just for Christmas Day.'

I couldn't give in to her on this one. I still couldn't forgive him for his relationship with her when she was under-age. The rest of the family wouldn't accept him either.

In the end we decided that Fi would spend Christmas morning with Elroy and then I would pick her up at lunch-time for the rest of the day. I would take her back down to Elroy's in the evening.

We didn't know then that this was to be Fiona's last Christmas. As a child she had always loved Christmas and would spend ages planning presents and cards for everyone. This time she threw herself into making a wonderful occasion for Elroy to remember. I gave her an old artificial tree from the attic and they decorated it with lots of trimmings. To my surprise Elroy acquired some sparkling lights. The next time I visited, Fi proudly showed me their efforts. The flat did indeed look very festive.

We still have Christmas stockings in our family, so I made one up for Fi to have with her on Christmas Eve. I felt sad when I thought that this would be the first time ever she wouldn't be opening it with us on Christmas morning. Fiona decided that Elroy too must have a stocking. My heart softens when I think of this thirty-four-year-old thief and drug-taker having his Christmas stocking hung up for him by my innocent daughter who, at sixteen, could only see the good in him. I found her shopping list for that stocking among her possessions after her death.

Fiona did not see another Christmas. The following year we all thought it very strange that she made no preparations at all. She was murdered on 17 December 1993. It was the first Christmas ever that she hadn't anticipated with great pleasure. I think she had lost interest in earthly pleasures by then and her spirit was preparing for a new life.

*

It was during this period that I decided that a move away from Totley would be sensible. There were many reasons: the house was large and old; it required constant upkeep and I didn't have the time or money to spend on it; the garden was too large for me to manage by myself. I thought that I could improve my financial situation by moving to a smaller house with a reduced mortgage.

There was another reason. By now, Fi was well and truly labelled in Totley and her reputation was affecting Rebecca and John. We all agreed that a move would be a good idea and the children began to look forward to a fresh start somewhere else.

Having said this, I did have many many good friends in the neighbourhood: those who wrote to me after Fiona died; those who turned up on my doorstep with food and flowers; those who loved and cared for my family and remain our true friends. There were also many people I didn't know very well who came up to me in the street, expressed their sorrow and said, 'It could have been any of our children,' even if secretly they thought, 'That would never happen to my child.'

To these people I owe a debt of gratitude. Their kindness and compassion started me on the road to recovery. They showed me, at a time when I desperately needed to see, that there was love and caring in the world, more than enough to combat the evil deed perpetrated by Zebbi and Duffy.

I still thought that, on balance, a fresh start would be

best. The house was subsequently put on the market and we looked forward eagerly to the move. Like many other properties at that time, it attracted some interest but we were slow in finding a buyer. It seemed pointless to look for a house to buy ourselves until we were certain of a sale, so we decided that when we did eventually find a buyer, we would rent a house for a few months. This would give us a breathing space and also put us in a good position as buyers.

After Christmas I sensed that life down at Broomhall was beginning to pall a little for Fiona. The owner of Porkys had to close the café, apparently as a result of financial problems, shortly after the black eye episode, so Fiona no longer had a job.

Money was tight, and Elroy had started stealing again, despite Fi's best efforts to turn him into a law-abiding citizen. Fiona hated his thieving.

One evening she came home and asked if she could stay for a few nights.

'Of course you can. You don't have to ask, Fi,' I assured her.

'This is your home.'

Then she told me what had happened. 'Elroy's in prison, Mum. He was on bail for one offence, and then the police arrested him again. They caught him up the driveway of this person's house. He told them that he was just looking for somewhere to relieve himself, but they wouldn't believe him.'

'That's hardly surprising,' I said wryly.

'Mum,' Fi insisted. 'They thought that he was going to burgle the house but he has never done a burglary. They were wrong to arrest him. He isn't a burglar. He's what's called an opportunist thief.'

'Whatever he is,' I muttered, 'he shouldn't be doing it at all.'

'They shouldn't have put him in prison but he's got to stay there until next week when it will come to court. Mum, will you come down to the court with me? I don't want to go on my own and I want to be there for him.'

I felt so sorry for her suddenly, that I agreed. 'OK, I can have a morning off work and come with you.'

'Thanks, Mum,' she said happily, giving me a hug.

On the due day we set off for the courthouse and were directed to the right room. They couldn't tell us at exactly what time Elroy's case would be heard, so we sat there and listened to a few petty offences being dealt with. Then it was Elroy's turn. He was led into the dock and the charge against him was read out.

'Mr Bishop,' the magistrate addressed him. 'I understand that you have dispensed with the services of your solicitor and intend to defend this matter yourself?'

'He wasn't any good,' Elroy replied. 'I shouldn't be in prison. I know my rights. I wasn't doing anything wrong when I was arrested. That solicitor they gave me doesn't know his job.' He continued in this vein for a while longer, ending up with, 'I'm in prison because I'm black, that's the only reason.'

The magistrate regarded him over the top of his glasses. 'Mr Bishop,' he said, firmly but kindly. 'I think you should reconsider this. If you are unhappy with the solicitor who has spoken to you, we should be able to arrange for you to see someone else. It really would be in your best interest.'

Elroy considered this for a moment and then agreed to give it a go with an alternative defence solicitor. The case was adjourned until the afternoon.

I couldn't wait with Fi to hear the outcome as I had to return to work. When I got home at tea-time she was waiting for me with a big grin on her face.

'I told you he shouldn't have been put in prison,' she said jubilantly. 'They released him straight away in the afternoon. I'm going back down to stay with him tonight.'

Although Fiona was happy that Elroy was out of prison, I could tell that she was getting really fed up. She started to spend a lot more time at home and would often mix with Rebecca and some of her young friends. Then there occurred a very unpleasant incident which provided the final impetus for her to leave Broomhall and return home for good.

One afternoon, Fi was talking to Sandra outside her flat when they were joined by Yvonne, the young girl who had broken Fi's nose the previous year. There was by now an uneasy truce between these two. It is possible that Fi had earned some respect by not 'grassing' on Yvonne to the police. In the event there had been no further trouble between them.

The three girls were soon joined by two young men. These men wanted Yvonne to meet them in the pub later on that evening and to bring Fiona along. Fi told me afterwards that she didn't like them and that she'd told Yvonne that she didn't want to go. In fact she came home that evening and spent some time with us.

The next morning she was confronted by an absolutely furious Yvonne.

'Fiona,' she screamed. 'Because you wouldn't go to the pub last night, I couldn't go on my own. Them men that we were supposed to meet were really mad and one of them has broken into my flat and taken my stereo. It was worth two hundred quid. It's all your fault and you're going to have to pay for it. We'll start with this.'

She grabbed Fi's hand and roughly pulled Elroy's ring from her finger. 'I'll give you a week to get the rest of the money. A hundred and fifty quid or I'm goin' to come and beat you up again and it'll be much worse than before.'

Fi was really scared of her. 'But I haven't got any money,' she protested.

'Well, you'd better find some and quick,' was the answer.

That very afternoon, Fi came home and announced

that she couldn't live down there any longer. She told me about Yvonne and how she had been threatened by her.

'She took my ring, Mum,' she sobbed. 'Please can I come home?'

'Fi, this has always been your home, you know that,' I replied. I was really delighted that she was coming back to live with us.

'What about Elroy?' I asked. 'What does he think about it?'

'Mum,' she admitted for the first time, 'Elroy is off his head most of the time. I'll always love him though. Could he come up to our house and see me here from time to time?'

'Oh Fi, please don't ask that. The answer still has to be "no". It's just not fair on Rebecca and John.'

It was a measure of her disillusionment with life down on the square that this time there was no protest. She had really had enough and she definitely wanted to come home, even if it meant she wouldn't see so much of Elroy.

That evening, I took her back to the flat to pick up some clothes. We had to sneak in. She was really frightened of bumping into Yvonne, despite my reassurances that I would handle that young lady should the need arise.

'She'll kill you, Mum. She's really vicious.'

'If she ever lays a finger on me, I'll make sure that she gets put away for a long time,' I said, with a bravado I was far from feeling.

Elroy was at the flat. I was shocked at his appearance. He lay back in his chair, giggling to himself stupidly.

'Take me to the Notting Hill Carnival, Irene,' he drawled.

'Shut up Elroy,' Fi muttered at him, embarrassed.

So we packed up her things, rescued Robert and Fringe from their place on the sideboard, and I drove her away from Broomhall for what I sincerely and fervently hoped would be the last time.

I really thought that we were over the worst when Fiona came home. It was April 1993. Spring was beginning and with it I felt a new hope that all would now be well with my family.

I had wondered whether Fi would go back down to Broomhall, but I needn't have worried. She remained far too frightened of Yvonne to venture down there. Quite soon afterwards Elroy had to appear in court again on yet another charge. This time his luck had run out. I presume that there is a limit to the number of times you can do community service, and Elroy had reached that point. In the early summer of that year, he was given an eighteen-month sentence and taken to the Wolds Prison in Humberside to start paying his debt to society.

It was lovely to have my daughter back with us. We were a whole family again. Fi also seemed very keen to stop smoking draw and as far as I am aware she was not actually physically addicted to any hard drugs at that point. Even now I am still uncertain as to how many of her problems were caused by drugs. She was certainly, during the time she lived with Elroy, a very heavy user of marijuana. She had also tried other drugs. She had told me that she had tried crack and that she had also taken methadone, the heroin substitute. However when she came home that year, there were no obvious signs of withdrawal, as one would expect if she had been addicted to any of these substances. She did tell me that she occasionally suffered from palpitations and panic attacks, but these didn't seem to cause her undue distress. As she refused to seek medical advice, I presumed that this was not a major problem for her.

Fi and I discussed her future. She had no qualifications, having not been to school since she was fourteen. She was now seventeen.

'I really would like to do something like law, Mum,' she told me.

'I'd be able to help people like Elroy or I could specialise in ethnic minorities, or in cases where women are discriminated against.'

I knew she'd been fascinated by her attendance at court when Elroy had had to appear there. I was also well aware that she had a very fine brain and that the academic content of such a training would not pose great difficulties for her. Her main problems were of a social nature. Would she be able to overcome her fears of being bullied again? Could she stay away from drugs and the friends who advocated a lifestyle completely outside the norms for our society?

'Fi, that would be really wonderful,' I enthused. 'It would be so interesting and you could do it if you really wanted to. You can do anything if you're prepared to work at it.'

'I want to have a go, Mum,' she said.

So we decided that the best thing for her to do would be to get a job throughout the summer and then to apply to one of the tertiary colleges for a place on a full-time GCSE course in September.

We sat down together and went through the *Yellow Pages* picking out cafés – some of them solely vegetarian – and Fi wrote to them all. She described herself as a student hoping to go to college in the autumn and looking for work as a waitress until then. A few days later she was delighted to get a phone call from one of the owners of a café in a local park, asking her to call down for an informal interview. The park was only a short bus ride from our home and seemed ideal.

The next day I took her down to the café and we sat and chatted with the owners. Pat and Jane were two enterprising young women who had turned this café in the park into a successful business. They liked Fiona and offered her a job starting immediately.

That last summer of Fi's was a happy one. It almost seems like a gift to me now. If she had been murdered while she was living away from home, my last memories of her would have been of all the stress and unhappiness that she had endured at Broomhall. I was not privy to her happiest moments with Elroy down there, although I knew that their love for each other had given her many memories to hold and treasure.

As it was, my child had come home before she was taken from me and for this small token I am grateful.

Fi was happy working in the café. She was conscientious and worked hard. I myself washed up there a few times to help out on busy Sundays. She started to look healthier although she never managed to put on any weight. Fi often used to complain about her skinniness. The other women in the café tried really hard to fatten her up, feeding her all sorts of fattening goodies but to no avail. Mars Bar Toasties were a favourite. Fi made these revoltingly sweet toasted sandwiches for John and Rebecca at home as well.

The women in the café also mothered another girl, Anna, who helped out in the kitchen. She and Fiona became close friends over that summer. They spent a lot of their spare time together, talking and giggling. Fi also made other young friends during this period and they'd chat in the park and occasionally go to one of the nightclubs in town.

When she wasn't working, Fi spent quite a lot of time with Rebecca and some of her friends. Although there was three years' difference between them, the gap didn't seem to matter.

One hot Sunday, Fi, Rebecca and one of Rebecca's friends went out to Padley Gorge, a local beauty spot in

Derbyshire. Totley is on the edge of the Peak District and it's only a ten-minute drive into some quite picturesque scenery. Padley Gorge is a popular area for picnicking. Families regularly spend Sundays there. It had been a frequent haunt of ours when the children were young. There are some beautiful walks; wide stretches of moorland are intersected by a babbling brook which occasionally forms deep pools, bounded by boulders.

When I went to pick the three girls up this particular Sunday, they were happy and animated.

'What have you been up to then?' I asked, pleased to see them so exuberant.

'We've had a great time,' Rebecca said, laughing.

'We found this lovely little pool and we've been skinny dipping.'

The other two shrieked with laughter at their own behaviour.

'Did anybody see you?' I asked.

'We don't think so, but we weren't really bothered.'

I had to smile to myself. I imagined these three nymphs, swimming and splashing in the sunshine, oblivious to the proximity of the Sunday picnickers. They were enjoying themselves so much, feeling at one with nature.

Another gift for Fi. Another good and happy experience. I am so glad that she had times like these. She may have only had seventeen years but she lived them to the full.

As our dentist wrote to me after she died: 'Fiona was never boring.'

It was true. Every waking moment of her life was lived to the utmost. It was almost as if she was saying, 'I know I haven't got long so while I'm here I'll savour every moment. I'll put a lifetime into my short allotted span.'

Although I had hoped that all connections with the Rastafarians might be severed when Fi came back to live at home, it was not to be. She remained for the rest of her life a believer in Rastafarianism. She read her bible continually. I have never seen a young person so absorbed in the Old Testament and the Psalms. She would frequently point out passages to me which were a revelation for her.

'Please, Mum, will you read the bible,' she would beg.

I tried and still am trying to do so.

Nor had she given up on her dream of going to Africa, but for a while she was more realistic about it. As Elroy was locked away in prison, she was either going to have to wait for him or find a new soul mate to go with.

Music, a big part of Fi's life, was always in the Rastafarian tradition. The sounds of Bob Marley filled our house when she was at home. She saw in him a man with many spiritual qualities.

Fi only seemed to see the good in people. I used to

think this was a sign of her innocence. I often puzzle over it now. In truth, I think we are all capable of good and bad deeds. Whereas I would always worry about the effect a person's negative actions would have on my family, Fi looked for the positive.

'Bob Marley had about six different "wives" and God knows how many children,' I would point out to her. 'Most of the time he was completely stoned.'

'Mum, he was great,' she would insist. 'Just listen to his music and hear what he's saying. When he went back to Jamaica he never forgot his roots. All the street children came out to play with him and he loved them. All of his women and children are well looked after.'

Fi videoed a TV programme about Marley's life and watched it often. His early death fascinated her. She would watch his funeral procession with tears streaming down her face.

'Listen to his song, Mum. Listen.'

And I would hear Bob singing his own funeral march: 'Fly away home to Zion. Fly away home. One bright morning when my work is over, I'm goin' to fly away home.'

Well, his work was over at thirty-three, when he died of cancer.

I like to think of Fiona jammin' it up with him. It would be heaven for her, singing, dancing and screaming with delight. Maybe somewhere up there, in another realm, their spirits will touch. It's a nice thought and one of the images I use when I am haunted by visions of how she died.

That fine summer of 1993 eventually ended. We were all pleased when we finally found a buyer for our house and could start looking for somewhere to rent on a temporary basis. There was no rush as we understood the whole proceedings would take about twelve weeks.

In the meantime, if Fi was going to go to college, we needed to sort out a suitable course for her. She decided on Castle College, near the centre of town. They were able to offer a full-time GCSE course over the period of a year. She enrolled and chose five subjects: English, maths, psychology, sociology and law.

At the time she seemed to be quite happy and indeed even enthusiastic about the prospect. Just once I sensed she was wavering a little when she said, 'Mum, do you think I might be better off carrying on working at the café? It is a job and I'm lucky to have one these days.'

I wasn't sure whether or not she'd be able to stay on at the café. She was originally employed just to work through the summer holidays, the café's busiest time. I said this to her and also pointed out that she might regret it later on in life if she didn't seize the chances of education which were available to her now, when she was a free agent with only herself to think about.

Fi was friendly with another girl who also wanted to do some GCSEs and they arranged to go to the college together for their interview. I took them down in the car. I should have realised then that it wasn't going to be easy. There were groups of girls laughing and chatting in the college entrance.

'Mum, they're all laughing at me,' Fi wailed.

To my surprise my big 17 year old girl who had lived and survived amongst criminals and drug addicts in Broomhall, was frightened and close to tears.

The lesson that Fi was teaching me is really only becoming clearer now. Her friends in Broomhall had shown her great love and kindness. I could only see the bad side of their characters, where she appreciated the good in them. And as she had received only unkindness at the hands of many people who would be more respected in our society, she was terrified by these law-abiding members of our community. Whose is the greater sin? I do not know.

Fi managed to pull herself together and got through the interview. The head of the GCSE course turned out, very fortunately, to be the son of a friend of mine, who I had worked with for many years. He was extremely kind to Fi once she had explained her fears and her past experience of being bullied at school. He reassured her that college would be different.

'We don't have bullies here,' he told us. 'They're warned once and then, if their behaviour continues, they're out. It's not like school, which they have to attend. If you have any problems, you must come straight to me or your year tutor. It doesn't matter what it is, if you're worried, you've got to tell us about it and we'll do our best to help.'

Fiona came away a little happier, but I should have realised then how bad the damage was. Oh, that she had left her damned education! What do a few GCSEs matter? I would far rather have my child working in a café for the rest of her life, but alive.

All the same, as the beginning of term approached, we shopped for pens, pencils, folders, files and a new school bag. Fi finished working full time in the café but carried on doing it as a Saturday job for a short while. Towards the middle of September she started college. Initially she seemed to be managing.

In the meantime the house sale was going ahead and I was looking for somewhere to rent. I had decided that six months would be long enough for us to find the right house to buy. Having nothing to sell, we would be in a good position.

What quirk of fate drew me to Fenwick Road? Why, oh why was there such a beautiful property for rent there at a price we could afford? Number 19 was an elegant old detached stone house with four bedrooms, which meant we could have a bedroom each for the first time ever. There was loads of room and it was very comfortable. It had a modern kitchen with luxurious fitted units; the kids gasped when they saw it. It also had a spacious living room with a real coal fire. It seemed to be an ideal base from which we could search for a permanent home.

There was one drawback, which at the time I dismissed as unimportant. Fenwick Road was also the home of the parents of the Rastafarian, Zebbi, the very same Zebbi who had kept Fi away from our home for two nights when she was only fourteen.

I really didn't think that Fi would ever have anything to do with him again. Nor, for one minute, did I think he would be actually living at home with his parents. If ever Fi spoke about him it was in derogatory terms. She told me that she really disliked him. Fool that I was, I believed her. It was to turn out to be the worst mistake I have ever made in my entire life. At that time I honestly did not think he posed any threat to Fiona. How could I have been so wrong?

Shortly after I had signed the contract to move into Fenwick Road Fi admitted that all was not well at college. She confessed that she had been skipping classes. She was really upset.

'I can't manage it, Mum,' she said. 'I keep getting terrible panic attacks and I feel sick all the time. There are all these girls and they keep giving me dirty looks.'

She cried, desolate.

'I can't face it any longer. I feel as if everybody is laughing at me. I haven't got any friends there. It's not too bad in the lessons but dinner times are terrible. I've been walking around town on my own instead of going into the dining room.'

My heart went out to her. 'It's OK, love,' I reassured her. 'It really doesn't matter. You can get GCSEs any time you like, even when you're forty.'

I know that she was very relieved at my reaction. We discussed what to do and decided that she should look for a job once we had moved into Fenwick Road. I suggested that she might like to consider going for some counselling and she agreed to think about it.

Fi was very distressed at her inability to complete the college course. When we talked about it, she said that nobody had actually been nasty to her or intimidated her. She realised that her imagination was going into overdrive and we both knew that this was a direct consequence of her experiences at school. It made her very angry.

'I want to be able to do something with my life, but how can I? If only bullies knew what they were doing to people. They should be made to suffer like I have.'

So it was that we moved into Fenwick Road. Fiona was at her lowest ebb. Circumstances could not have been more favourable for Zebbi. When he realised how attractive Fiona had become he quickly seized his chance. We moved on 15 October. Fiona had two months left to live.

I read somewhere that the two most stressful events in our lives are getting a divorce and moving house. I thought to myself, 'Well, I've done both of those and I'm still standing, so I must be quite resilient, even if I don't feel it at times.' We were excited at the prospect and our cheerfulness helped. I went through the Totley house ruthlessly, throwing out or selling at car boot sales everything we didn't need. It was still quite a task as we seemed to have accumulated a mass of possessions during the years in Totley, and nothing would persuade the children to abandon any of their childhood toys.

We settled into 19 Fenwick Road and enjoyed the comfort and extra space. I particularly liked the lovely cosy family atmosphere from the real fire and lit it often in the evenings when we were at home together.

Fiona, though, was dispirited. I was aware of this and did my best to cheer her out of it. She enjoyed cooking and would often make our evening meal. Her vegetable casserole and dumplings became famous. She immersed herself even more into her bible reading and kept it by her side wherever she was in the house.

I was concerned that she was withdrawing into herself. She would spend hours poring over the Littlewoods and Empire catalogues. I have an exercise book which she filled at the time. In it she has written details of furniture, curtains, towels, bedclothes, etc., all neatly listed. I think she was daydreaming and planning how she would furnish a home of her own one day.

She also told me that she had a very strong feeling that she had lived before. 'I was an African princess, Mum,' she said. 'I was captured and they made me into a slave and then they killed me.'

I'm afraid I laughed at her. It seemed like just another of her notions, but she was convinced that she had lived before.

I had taken some time off work while we moved, but in early November I had to go back. I didn't want to leave Fiona on her own, but I had little choice. Around this time I was beginning to suspect that she was smoking marijuana again, and maybe using other drugs too. I was so tired and downhearted. It felt like torture. After all we'd been through, surely she wasn't going to go down that path again. I didn't know whether or not I had the strength to cope.

One night I got down on my knees and prayed. It went like this: 'Dear God, I don't know whether you are real or not, but if you do exist I am so sorry for doubting you. Please, please, will you put a stop to all this heartache of Fi's. I feel as if I can't go on any more. Please will you help me.'

In a way my prayer was answered, but it wasn't the way I would have chosen. Fi's searching was certainly soon ended and her heartache finished, as she left this earthly existence behind and went to a much better place.

My suspicions were soon confirmed. I noticed a change in Fi's appearance. She got very thin again and often looked white and ill, just as she had when she lived with Elroy. Then, to my dismay, another young man with dreadlocks and the regulation red, green and gold crocheted cap appeared on our doorstep. Fi introduced him and then went out with him for the evening.

Soon afterwards she started expounding Rastafarian dogma once more.

'Mum, I really can't stand the greed and corruption in our society today. I want to go to the land which Jah has given to those righteous people who don't want to be part of this dreadful Babylon.'

She was referring to the Rastafarian settlement in Ethiopia. In exasperation I said to her, 'Look, if you have a dream, you must try and do something to make your dream come true. Go out and get yourself a job and start saving. If you can save up two-thirds of your fare out there, I'll give you the rest.'

Really, I was calling her bluff. I didn't for one minute believe that she would want to go all that way, so far from her family, on her own. But when she heard my promise, her eyes lit up. She was delighted. Later on I learned that she had told one of her friends that I was going to help her get to her promised land.

I offered to go down to the job centre with her to help her look for a job. One afternoon I took her down in the car and we started to look at the vacancies. To my amazement, Fi suddenly began to act in a very weird fashion.

Picking up one of the cards, she said angrily – and loud enough for everyone to hear: 'Just look at this job. It's slavery. I'm not going to work in this white man's society. I don't want any part of it. It's Babylon.'

Heads turned until the whole room seemed to be looking at us. She shouted some more along the same lines while I, embarrassed and annoyed, tried to hustle her out of there.

'I thought you wanted a job,' I yelled at her in the car. 'Why do you have to make such a fool of us?'

She didn't have anything to say. I was puzzled as well as angry: I couldn't understand what was going on in her mind. I think Fi was also thoroughly confused, but I didn't know how to help her.

In mid November one of my aunts in Dublin was diagnosed as terminally ill with cancer. I decided to take my mother over there to see her sister one last time before she died. We arranged that my ex-husband would take care of the children while I was away.

At the last minute Fi announced that she was going

to stay with the sister of her new Rastafarian friend. She was seventeen and I couldn't stop her.

My mother and I flew to Dublin and spent three days with my aunt. It was a sad trip but we could see that she was at peace and more than ready to go from this life. She was not in pain and we returned home satisfied that all was as it should be for her.

When I got back home I was surprised to find Fiona at the house waiting for me.

'Mum, I've had an awful time,' she said. 'That man's sister wasn't there. He is quite mad. You'll never guess what happened.'

My heart sank as she told me all about it.

'He made me get down on my hands and knees and sweep through his house with a dustpan and brush. Even when it was perfectly clean, I had to do it over and over. When he went out he locked me in. I was really frightened but I managed to climb out of a window on to a garage roof and escape.'

'Fi,' I beseeched her, 'are you never going to learn?'

In the middle of our conversation the phone rang. It was her Rastafarian friend and he was furious. 'Fiona,' he yelled, 'you'd better get yourself back here within the hour or I'm coming over there to get you.'

Fi was terrified and so, for that matter, was I. I rang the police, who said that nothing could be done unless he came around to the house and actually started threatening us on the doorstep.

'Don't worry. If he arrives at your house, dial 999 and we'll be round to you straight away.'

I had to leave it at that. For the next couple of hours we sat there waiting to see if this man was going to carry out his threat. I had a feeling that he was simply trying to frighten Fi, but nevertheless it was an uncomfortable evening that we spent. I was relieved when night fell and he hadn't turned up.

After this episode we again sat down and talked. I repeated my suggestion of counselling. Fi agreed it would be useful to talk to someone outside the family but she wanted to find someone herself. I was pleased and thought it best to leave it up to her. I know she did contact somebody from one of the youth services and kept at least one appointment. I didn't want to pry, but she volunteered the information that she'd been told she was quite normal and shouldn't worry too much about her feelings. I think that she often doubted her own sanity and was relieved to get this reassurance.

Towards the middle of November, I overheard Fi talking about Zebbi. She just mentioned very casually that she had spotted him at his mother's house up the road. I thought nothing of it at the time.

Once when we were returning home from town she pointed out his car, parked outside his house. It was easy to recognise as the number plate was broken. Then I noticed that it was often parked up the road. Shortly afterwards there was a toot on a horn outside our house and Fi went running out. I went to the window and saw her getting into Zebbi's car.

It happened frequently then. It was always the same. There would be a toot on the horn, at any hour of the day or evening, and the next minute Fi would go running out to him. At first she would only be gone for a short while, but gradually she was spending more and more time with him. To say I was unhappy about it would be an understatement. When I asked Fi about him she was reluctant to say much. Then one evening he took her out clubbing. The next day, eyes shining, she told me all about it.

'We had a smashing time. Zebbi knows lots of the musicians and they all know him. He introduced me to lots of people. I met Lieutenant Stitchie. Mum, I've had the most fantastic time. I've been dancing all night.'

'Who the heck is Lieutenant Stitchie?' I asked.

She laughed. 'He's a reggae singer. You'd like him.'

Suddenly Fi's life seemed to be spiralling out of control. Sometimes she had only just come in when there would be a toot on the horn and she would dash straight out again, no matter what hour of the day or night it was. She was like a whirlwind. She seemed to be existing on very little sleep. I don't know where she got the energy from. I had very strong suspicions that she must be using some sort of stimulant. I already knew she was back on the 'holy herb' with a vengeance.

One evening I became very depressed about the

whole situation. I went into Fiona's room and found a bottle of very expensive-looking whisky. Goodness knows where she had got it from. On a sudden impulse I took it down to the kitchen and drank some. About forty minutes later I had finished the lot and was beyond caring. It was probably about half a bottle, but I hadn't been in the habit of drinking more than a small amount of alcohol for ages, and I was quite drunk.

It was still only early evening, so I took it into my head to go for a short walk to try and sober up. As I came back down Fenwick Road I suddenly noticed Zebbi looking into his car. Fi wasn't with him. As I passed the car, I had an overwhelming desire to insult him. In my still drunken state I couldn't think of anything suitably scathing, so I just said, 'Good evening, Edward,' in what I thought was a sneering voice. For some reason I thought that if I called him by his very English name and not his Rastafarian title he'd be able to feel my contempt for him.

He looked up with surprise, but said nothing, so I carried on home.

This incident was to have some repercussions. A few days later I was at home with Fi when there was a ring on the doorbell. Fi opened it and after a few minutes appeared in the kitchen with Zebbi.

He approached me. 'I think we should be friends,' he said. 'I felt awful when you walked by the car the other day and said "Good evening", and I never even replied.'

I couldn't believe what I was hearing. Talk about

incidents rebounding on you! He had thought I was being nice to him. It certainly served me right. I was stunned into silence.

Eventually I muttered something to the effect of 'We'll see how it goes', and left them together.

A few minutes later Fi told me that she was going out for a drive with him. As she went upstairs for her coat, he lounged on the bottom of the stairs waiting for her. I was instantly reminded of a picture of Satan which I must have seen in my childhood. For a moment his dreadlocked hair reminded me of coiled serpents and I had a strong feeling that this man was representative of much that was wicked and bad in the world. The wickedness I sensed in him frightened me.

I didn't know then why I was so repulsed by Zebbi, or that my intuition that he was going to harm my family was right. In a way I was surprised at the depth of my dislike. His actions were, as far as I knew at the time, certainly no worse than Elroy's, yet I had never felt this way about Elroy. Indeed we had all come to have a soft spot for him. Fi still professed to love him and wrote to him in prison.

One night at the beginning of December, Fi didn't come home. She didn't phone me either so I was concerned, but I decided to wait until the morning before alerting the police.

The next day was a Saturday so we were all at home.

I got up early and lit a fire which was soon glowing cosily in the living room. Fi's friend from the café, Anna, called round and we were just having tea and toast in front of the fire when Fi arrived. Her face was white and strained and her eyes looked dead. We all stared at her and I was shocked at how ill she looked.

'Fi, love, what's happened to you? Where have you been?'

'I'm all right, Mum. Don't make a fuss.'

She greeted Anna and they chatted for a few minutes. But I could tell that Anna too was upset by her appearance. Eventually she told us what she had been doing.

'Last night I went down to the pub on the square and had a drink with some friends. One of them gave me some morphine tablets and I took them. Then I had some beer and I remember feeling really sick. Somebody took me outside and then I can't remember anything else that happened. I woke up in this strange flat in Broomhall this morning and then I came straight home.'

We all looked at her sadly.

'Fi,' I said. 'If you don't stop behaving like this, I'm going to be identifying you on a cold slab in some hospital morgue somewhere.'

I didn't know then how prophetic my words were going to turn out to be. Less than two weeks later that was precisely what I was doing in Doncaster's Royal Infirmary.

We all chatted for a while. Fi had some tea with lots of sugar. She stretched out in front of the fire and the colour started to come back into her cheeks.

Suddenly from outside we heard the wretched sound of Zebbi's car horn.

'Don't go out, Fi,' I begged her. 'Anna's come all the way over to see you. Tell him you'll see him later.'

'I can't, Mum,' she replied. 'I'm really sorry, Anna. I've got to go. I'll see you later.'

With that she was off. She behaved as if he was her master. During those last weeks, whatever she was doing, no matter how ill or tired she felt, when his car appeared at the door, she ran to him.

The following Saturday, a week before she died, we were at home together, just the two of us. I was cooking in the kitchen when Fi came up to me. She was looking very thoughtful.

'Mum,' she said, 'I am so miserable here, but don't worry about me. I haven't got much longer.'

'Fi, please don't talk like that,' I said. 'What can I do to help you? How can we make things better for you?'

'You can't do anything, Mum. I will never be happy in this life. I can't wait to go from here and it won't be long now.' She was holding her bible as she spoke.

I looked at her. She made me want to cry. 'Fi, you're not going to die. You feel like this because of the drugs you've been taking. They twist your mind. You don't know what you're doing or saying half the time.'

'No, Mum, you're wrong,' she said. 'All my life I've known that I wouldn't live to be old. I've told you before but you never listen to me. I am not happy here but I haven't got much longer, so it doesn't matter.'

I've thought about this conversation many times since. I know now that at that time she had already been coerced into prostitution by Zebbi. From my later reading of the transcript of the court case against Fiona's murderer – Duffy – I found out that she had worked on the street in Doncaster the previous night and again was seen there on the Saturday evening following this conversation. I think this must have been the cause of her misery. Maybe she was trying to tell me what she had been doing. Very rarely had she kept any of her previous exploits from me, but this was one she would have been deeply ashamed to tell me about.

I also believe that she did have a strong premonition about what was going to happen to her. She must have known by then that Zebbi was a bad man. It seems as if she believed that destiny had drawn them together and there was no way she could escape. I just felt desolate and hopeless for her, powerless to help.

It was getting close to Christmas and despite all our problems I was determined to make an effort, though my heart was not really in it. We bought a small tree and trimmed it. For the first time ever Fi wasn't interested. She made no shopping lists. She wasn't bothered about helping me to plan a menu for Christmas Day. She bought no presents. That last week of her life she was rarely at home. She told me Zebbi was taking her to a club in Doncaster every night.

I was very concerned about her. She wasn't working. It did cross my mind that she had no money of her own apart from the occasional fiver that I slipped her. I had absolutely no idea that she was working the streets for Zebbi, on one occasion earning as much as £200 in one evening. What she did with this money, I really don't know; she certainly never had any herself. One evening she came in with a new white skimpy Lycra top. She told me Zebbi had bought it for her. I can only assume that most of what she earned went towards supplying Zebbi's cravings for drugs.

One evening in that last week, Rebecca and I were chatting about things in general when she suddenly turned to me with a troubled look and said, 'Mum, Fiona told me that the other night when she went to Doncaster with Zebbi, he went and collected some money off some prostitutes who were working on the street there.'

'Rebecca, she never said that really, did she?' I asked in amazement.

'She did, Mum, honest. She told me not to tell you, so please don't say I've told you.'

'I'll have to say something to her, Rebecca. That's awful.'

'Why does she have to go out with him?' Rebecca

moaned. 'I can't stand him. He's awful.'

I tried to soothe her: 'Don't worry. I'm sure she'll soon get tired of him.' It was said with a confidence I was far from feeling at the time.

When Fi came in later that night, I tackled her with what Rebecca had told me.

'That's not true,' she gasped. 'Rebecca's only saying that because she doesn't like him.'

'Fi, please will you tell me the truth?'

'Honest, Mum, I am telling the truth,' she insisted. 'I bet she said that because you're not happy about her seeing Gary.' (I was a bit wary of Rebecca's friend Gary, but compared to Zebbi, he was an angel.)

I had to let it go at that, as just then there was a knock on the door. It was Zebbi. He asked if he could speak to Fiona on her own and the two of them disappeared upstairs to her bedroom. They were only a few minutes. I don't know what he said to her but when they came down, Fi looked very subdued and worried, as if she'd had a good telling off. Late as it was they went out together, Fi telling me not to wait up as she went out of the door.

I don't know why I didn't believe what Rebecca told me. And I shall never know why Fi didn't tell me the truth about what was happening, though it's clear now that Zebbi had got a hold over her, and that she was very scared of him. Maybe she realised that she'd finally crossed the line and was afraid that she'd lose my support, that I'd throw her out of the house. Certainly I would have had great difficulty coming to terms with it. If she was going to carry on living with us at home, she would have had to escape from Zebbi's influence. Maybe she'd just given up.

The fact remains: I didn't know what Fi was doing at the time even if now, with hindsight, it seems to have been staring me in the face.

The day before Fiona died, I noticed that the poker was missing from its usual place by the fireside. Later on in the day, I found it under Fi's bed. She was obviously very frightened of someone.

The morning of 17 December dawned cold and bright. Fi was in bed when I left that morning to go to work. Part way through the morning I received a telephone call from Dublin to say that my aunt was critically ill and not expected to last the day. I took the rest of the day off work and drove to my mum's flat to pick her up and bring her across to Fenwick Road to await further news. No sooner had we arrived home than the phone rang. My aunt had died. My mum was naturally upset and we spent the rest of the afternoon together.

Rebecca and John arrived home and we had some tea. Fiona, who had also been out somewhere, eventually arrived. I remember that she came in quite noisily, so I motioned her to be quiet and told her about my aunt. She went over to my mum at once and gave her a big hug.

'Granny, I'm really sorry,' she said and they chatted for a while.

At about seven my mum said she'd like to go back to her own flat so we prepared to go.

'I'm just dropping Granny off and then I'll be back. I won't be long,' I shouted to the kids.

At that very moment Zebbi's car pulled up outside and Fiona grabbed her jacket.

'Mum, I may not be here when you get back,' she said. 'I'm going clubbing in Doncaster with Zebbi. I'll be staying out very late tonight.'

'I'll see you when I see you then,' I replied.

That was all. As simple as that. The last time I saw my daughter alive. Why, oh why wasn't there a fanfare of trumpets to herald that moment? Why couldn't I have hugged and kissed her and feasted my eyes on her living breathing body? I would have savoured each moment so much, if I had only known it was to be the last.

Later that night Fiona lay dead in a miserable, lonely, top-floor car park. She lay there all night on her own, with no company but the lonely wail of the goods trains whistling through the depot below. Oh God, let her not have woken up to realise her plight before merciful death claimed her. Let her have been dead when her murderer left her.

The next morning, a Saturday, when I woke up and realised Fi wasn't home, I had no inkling of what had happened to her. I didn't feel too concerned. She had survived so many scrapes that I was beginning to feel that she must have a charmed life. At about midday, there was a phone call.

'Hi, it's Zeb,' said the voice on the other end. 'Is Fiona there?'

'No. I thought she was with you. Where is she?'

'I dropped her off last night in Sheffield,' he replied. 'I just wondered if she was at home.'

'Where did you drop her off? What time was it? Why didn't you bring her back here?' I was almost shouting at him.

'I dropped her off at the bottom of London Road. It was a bit before midnight.'

'Why on earth did you do that?' I asked. 'Why didn't you bring her home?'

'She said she was going to stay with some friends,' he said and he hung up.

Later on I was to discover that these were all lies. Zebbi had never brought Fiona back from Doncaster, where he'd taken her on Friday night. He couldn't have, because at the time he said he'd dropped her off in Sheffield, she was already dead in the car park in Doncaster.

After this telephone call I was uneasy, but thought that Fi might have gone down to stay with Sandra, who lived near the bottom of London Road. The rest of the day passed and I waited for her to come home. For some reason, I didn't see or hear any news or read any newspapers that day, unusual, as I'm quite a news addict. If I had seen that day's evening papers I would have been shocked to the core. The news that the body of a girl had been found in a Doncaster car park was reported widely. A computerised picture of Fiona's profile was printed in our local paper with the caption 'DO YOU KNOW THIS GIRL?' I am glad I didn't see it. Apparently one of Fi's friends had thought it might be her and then dismissed the idea as ridiculous.

When Fiona wasn't home by Saturday evening, I went looking for her. I called on her friends and then trawled the streets of Broomhall. I went into the two local pubs on the square with her photo. Nobody had seen her that weekend or knew where she was.

I returned home dispirited. Around 11.30 p.m. the phone rang. Rebecca picked it up. It was a man asking for Fiona. I motioned to Rebecca to hand me the phone but whoever it was had hung up.

'Who was it?' I asked Rebecca.

'It was Zebbi, Mum. I recognised his voice,' she said.

By now, Zebbi must have been very worried. He had obviously had to come back from Doncaster on the Friday night without her. Maybe he had seen the reports and was hoping frantically that it wasn't her. Maybe he thought she hadn't been able to meet him where they had arranged and would have made her own way home. He must have been praying that she'd be at home each time he rang.

The following day, Sunday, I resolved to contact the police if Fiona had not turned up by the evening. We had previously arranged to call upon the children's Nana in Leeds, our usual Christmas visit. I decided to go as arranged; if Fi wasn't home when we got back, then I'd inform the police.

Before we set out I thought I'd go up the road to Zebbi's house and ask him for more details about what Fi said she was going to do when he had supposedly dropped her off on the Friday night. I knocked on his door and his mother answered.

'Can I speak to Zebbi please?' I asked.

'I'm afraid he's in bed,' she said.

'I really must speak to him,' I insisted. 'I haven't seen my daughter, Fiona, since he took her out on Friday night.'

She looked worried. 'Just a minute, I'll go up and see if he's awake.'

I waited outside while she went upstairs. She wasn't very long. 'He's too tired to come down and speak to you. He says he doesn't know where Fiona is. I've looked under his bed and in his wardrobe and he hasn't got her hidden anywhere.' She laughed. 'I know what these young people are like.'

I wasn't amused. 'Please will you tell him that if Fiona isn't home this evening I'm going to inform the police.' With that I left.

I wondered if Zebbi's mother associated me with that same mother who had been looking for her fourteen-year-old daughter three years ago.

We spent a relaxed afternoon in Leeds and I tried for a while to forget my increasing anxiety. In the middle of the afternoon I rang home to see if Fi was back. To my relief the phone was engaged.

'Fi must be back,' I said to Rebecca. 'She's on the phone to one of her friends. She'll be cross she's missed coming to Leeds with us.'

My relief was short lived. There was no sign of Fi when we got home. The engaged tone when I rang home must have been some cruel coincidence, someone else trying to phone perhaps.

It was now Sunday evening. I couldn't wait any longer. One night without hearing from her I could take, but not two. She would have phoned me by now if she was able to. Something must be dreadfully wrong. I phoned the police to report her missing.

Fiona's Story

Within the hour two policemen in uniform arrived. I was familiar with the procedure although it had been a while since I had had to go through it. They took all the details, what she had been wearing, etc. I remembered she'd had on the white Lycra top Zebbi had bought her and a short black skirt with tights or leggings, I wasn't sure which. She also had a black jacket she had bought with money she earned at the café. I found some of her most recent photos. By chance, she had had some photos done by a professional photographer only a few months before. They were good photos and she had been delighted with them at the time.

When they had all the information they needed the officers left. By now it was getting late and we were all tired. Rebecca and John went to bed and were soon fast asleep. I made myself a cup of coffee and went up to my bedroom with the Sunday papers. It was then that I read that small article in the national newspaper.

The body of a young girl has been found in a multi-storey car park in Doncaster. It is believed to be the body of a young woman aged between 15 and 22 years. She had been badly beaten, and sexually assaulted.

That moment was the end of my life as I had known it. I knew instantly that it was Fiona. She fitted the description. I knew that Zebbi had taken her to

Doncaster. She had not arrived home.

I was sick to the very core of my being. My heart started to pound. I got on my knees and prayed that it wasn't her. But I knew with an awful certainty that it must be. How was I going to endure it?

A few minutes later the phone rang.

'Woodseats Police here, Is your daughter home yet?'

They too must think that they had found the identity of the body. Never once on all those other occasions when Fi was younger and I reported her missing had they phoned me back to see if she had turned up.

'No, she's not home,' I almost screamed. 'But I've just read about the young girl whose body has been found in a Doncaster car park. Has she been identified yet? I think it's my daughter.'

The voice on the other end of the phone tried to calm me. 'Don't panic. We're just doing all the routine checks.'

'Please tell me,' I begged. 'Have you identified the body in Doncaster yet?'

'No, we haven't,' he finally admitted. 'But please try and stay calm and let us know if your daughter contacts you.'

I was petrified. A bit of me kept thinking, 'It's not her. Things like this don't happen to people like me.' But a dreadful cold chill was starting to grip me as I realised that my worst nightmare was about to come true.

The phone rang again and I grabbed it.

'Yes,' I gasped.

'Mrs Ivison?'

'Yes?'

'It's Doncaster Police here. We're sending two officers over to talk to you.'

'Then it is my daughter,' I whispered.

'Please try and stay calm. Someone will be with you very shortly.'

'OK,' I answered and put the phone down.

I tried to control the sick feeling in the pit of my stomach. I couldn't do anything. I went downstairs, sat on the window sill and waited for them to arrive. I knew without a doubt that they were going to confirm my terrible fears. Fiona was dead.

I didn't have to wait long before the two officers arrived at Fenwick Road. By now it was about two o'clock in the morning. They were both tall and smartly dressed, Graham and Derek. Graham has since become a family friend. They were very kind.

As soon as they came in the door, I was saying to them, 'You don't have to tell me. I know it's my daughter in the car park.'

They came with me into the living room. Embers still glowed cosily in the fireplace. Derek sat with me on the sofa and Graham sat on an upright chair in the corner. These details are imprinted in my mind. I know that I will never forget that morning. Other memories fade but that scene stays as vividly as if it happened yester-day.

As soon as we were seated Derek asked, 'Can you remember any other identifying marks which Fiona has?'

I thought quickly. 'She had a small scar on her fore-head. She had a bump on her nose from when it was broken over a year ago.'

'Anything else?'

I tried hard to remember. 'She had a large mole under one of her breasts, I can't remember which one.'

This must have been what they were waiting for.

Derek placed his hand on my shoulder. 'I am very sorry, but I have to tell you that there is no doubt that the girl whose body has been found in Doncaster is your daughter.'

'Yes, I know,' was all I could say.

We sat in silence for a few moments.

'Tell me. How did she die?' I asked.

'She died from a head injury is all we can tell you at the moment.'

'I want to see her. When can I see her?'

'We do need someone to formally identify her. If you feel up to it we can take you over to Doncaster soon. Are you on your own in the house?'

'I have two teenagers who are asleep upstairs,' I told them.

'I'll come over in the morning and take you across

then,' Graham said. 'Would you like us to get a police-woman to come and stay with you for the rest of the night?'

I nodded. By now, I was in deep shock. Although I felt quite calm, I didn't think I could be left on my own. I might have gone mad.

Graham made us some coffee while we waited for the policewoman to arrive. I told them that Fiona had left our house on Friday evening with Zebbi and how he had been taking her to Doncaster regularly over the last two weeks. My first thoughts then were that he must have killed her and dumped her body in the car park. I gave them his address and they said they would speak to him in the morning.

Within a short time an attractive young policewoman in plain clothes arrived. Her name was Natalie. Graham and Derek left and she sat with me on the sofa. We didn't sleep. We sat and talked until the early morning light appeared. For such a young person, and in such distressing circumstances, Natalie was wonderful. She stayed every night with us for the next few days. When John and Rebecca couldn't sleep she would take them out in her car and go and buy pizza for them. I would find the three of them all cuddled up together on the sofa in the morning. Rebecca and John loved her. She and Graham did much to help us get through those early days.

Those hours in the morning were strange and unreal.

I remember thinking, 'The worst thing that I could ever imagine happening has happened to me, yet I am still here. I am still alive and I am still breathing. I haven't gone mad. If I can endure this pain, one minute at a time, I will cope.'

I knew I had to be strong for Rebecca and John, so I determined even then that we would recover. We had to go forwards. It was what Fiona would have wanted us to do.

In the morning Natalie rang Oakes Park physio department and told them I wouldn't be coming into work that day. I didn't wake Rebecca or John. There would be no school for them for a while. One of my very good friends at work, obviously concerned, rang straight back to see if there was anything wrong. She thought it must be something serious as I had not rung in myself.

Natalie asked me if I would like to speak to her. I took the phone.

'It's Fiona,' I stuttered. 'She's been murdered.'

There. I had said it. The words sounded stark and unreal. It was such a dreadful thing to have to say to anyone, and about your own child.

My friend on the other end of the phone drew in her breath in horror. 'Oh Irene. Oh no. Not Fiona.'

'Yes, I'm afraid so. They found her in a car park.'

'Not the one in Doncaster? Oh Irene, I'm so sorry.'

I couldn't manage to talk any more, so I rang off saying I would get in touch later on.

As I put the phone down I heard the sounds of muffled sobbing and then I saw my son John dash into his room. He had come to the top of the stairs and overheard me telling the dreadful news. I had not meant him to hear it like that. I went to him in his room and held him as he sobbed.

Oh, you blasted murderer. Did you not think of her family? What did we ever do to you? Did you not think she might have had a brother and a sister? Thirteen and fourteen. What would you say to them to explain what you did? Whatever in your life brought you to that place where you had to unleash your vengeance on our child, it was not our fault. Did you really think that Fiona was just a piece of shit that you could stamp out and no one would care? Did you think her life was so worthless and of so little importance?

Then I had to go and tell Rebecca.

Her screams will haunt me for the rest of my life.

'No, it's not true. Not Fiona.'

Then, as I held her and tried to tell her gently: 'It's Zebbi. Zebbi's killed my sister.'

Her heartrending screams seemed to go on for ever. I thought she would never stop. It crossed my mind that I should have thought of getting some tranquillisers from the doctor before I told her.

I realise now that Rebecca's reaction was healthy and

the best thing for her, certainly far better than filling her up with sedatives. It was hard for me to listen to, though. I was incensed that she should have to suffer like this. Adolescence is such a difficult time anyway. How were they going to cope with this terrible loss and the way it was done?

By this time Graham had returned to take me to the morgue. There were other things to do first though. We had a drink and he sat in the living room with us and we spoke a bit more about what had happened to Fiona. It must have been difficult for him. Apparently Fiona had last been seen walking away from a street in Doncaster's red light area. She was with a man the police were assuming was a client. Slowly it dawned on me what was being said. Fiona had been selling her body, working as a street prostitute in Doncaster on the night she died.

I buried my face in my hands while it sank in.

'I don't believe it,' I said.

'Mum, it's true.' This was Rebecca. 'She told me she was doing it. I'm sorry I didn't tell you. I know I should have told you. I heard Zebbi threatening her with a battering if she didn't get money for him. I heard him going on at her in our garden. He was shouting at her.'

She started to cry again. 'It's all my fault. It wouldn't have happened if I'd told someone. It's my fault Fiona's been killed.'

Oh, sorrow upon sorrow. Fiona exploited and sold on

the streets by a pimp and then murdered by a violent punter – and my fourteen-year-old daughter thinks it's her fault.

'Rebecca, it's not your fault.' I almost shouted it at her. 'How could it possibly have been your fault? I don't know what difference it would have made if I'd known what was going on. I probably wouldn't have been able to get her out of it. I would have made her leave home and then she might have died away from us, feeling unloved and unwanted, even by her own family. At least this way she knew we loved and cared about her.'

I held Rebecca as tightly as I could.

'Rebecca, I love you. I would never in a million years blame you for not telling me. I could say it's my fault for coming to live in the same street as Zebbi's parents. Tell me. How long was she doing it for?'

'Only for about two weeks, Mum.' Rebecca looked slightly relieved that I wasn't angry with her for keeping Fiona's secret. 'She told me the first night she did it. She said it wasn't as terrible as she thought it was going to be. She told me that she earned £200 in one night. Zebbi waited around the corner and she gave the money to him. Mum, she told me not to worry you about it.'

Poor Rebecca held this burden of guilt for a long time. I could never for one minute blame her for not telling me. She had, after all, told me about the night that Zebbi went to Doncaster and collected money from the other girls he had working the streets there, and I had chosen to believe Fiona when she denied it. If it was anybody's fault, it was mine for not being able to see what was staring me in the face.

The sense of guilt is hard to live with. But of course we are not to blame. A good deal of the fault lies with a society which allows children even to be called prostitutes. As far as I am concerned, any girl under eighteen working the streets in this way is not a prostitute. She is a victim of child sexual exploitation and should be protected, not vilified.

I am not ashamed of Fiona in any way, but I am ashamed of a society which does little to stop this exploitation. When I learned what she had been doing, I immediately thought of my family and the inevitable sensationalism. We were, after all, a 'decent middle-class family'. Then I realised that every woman who stands out there on a street and sells her body is a victim. Most of these women receive scant sympathy and are regarded by society as the lowest of the low. Yet what about the men who use them? Where are *their* names? Where is *their* loss of dignity and self-respect?

As I absorbed the truth of what Fi had been doing, it seemed to be just another sad fact to cope with. The most important thing to me then was to know how she had died. I hoped desperately that it had been quick.

Rebecca said to me later, 'Mum, do you know what I can't stand the thought of? I can't stand the thought of her being frightened.'

I understood then that this was what I too couldn't bear to face. I wondered if Fiona had realised that this was it; this was one situation she wasn't going to get out of.

Graham told me that her death had probably been quick. He said her injuries were consistent with her head being banged repeatedly on the concrete floor of the car park.

'She would have been instantly stunned,' he told me. 'She would not have known what was happening after that.'

Oh, how I wanted to believe him. It was the only consolation left to us now. I prayed that it was so and that she had not known the horror of her murderer's rage and seen the hate and anger in his face as he vented his fury on her.

The morning passed quickly at the house as we made practical arrangements. The children's father arrived, shocked and distraught at the news. We were told that the police were working flat out to find the murderer. We all had to give statements. It was decided that Rebecca and John would go with their father to a special unit that afternoon to tell all they knew of recent events. I would go with Graham to the mortuary in Doncaster to make a formal identification of Fiona's body. I was told that following my identification the news would be released to the press.

That afternoon I set off with Graham. Although I wanted to see her, I was worried about what she might look like. I was numb and shocked. There was no doubt in my mind that I should see her, but I felt I needed to be prepared for what I might have to face. Graham told me that she had a large area of discoloration down one side of her face. I asked him if there would be other bodies in the morgue. He looked a bit surprised at this question, but all I had ever seen of mortuaries was on TV, films where the body is pulled out of a drawer in a large cold room, full of cabinets housing other corpses.

I took with me my favourite photo of Fiona, to remind me how she was in life. I would look at what had been done to her in death but this was how I would remember her. I asked Graham if we could play Mozart's 'Exultate Jubilate' and other sacred music in the car. I desperately needed things that were good and beautiful around me, as if the evil of this crime would have to be combated in some way by the power of love and beauty.

When we arrived at Doncaster Royal Infirmary, we parked in a quiet area near the mortuary. We were met by a nurse and a man who I presumed was an attendant in the morgue. They took us down to a quiet room in the basement of the hospital.

I faltered a little as we approached and the nurse asked me, 'Would you like to look at her through the window first?'

'Yes, I would,' I said, and then we were at the window.

Fiona lay on a dais in the middle of this small room. She was shrouded in white. The marked side of her face was towards me.

'It's OK,' I said. 'I can go in now.'

I am not unfamiliar with death and I did not fear seeing the body of my child. How could she frighten me? She had loved me in life and known she was loved. Now she lay cold before me. Only her face was visible. The rest of her was swathed and coiffed in white. Her eyes were closed. I touched her smooth white face. There is no cold so cold as the chill of death.

'She's so cold,' I murmured.

I wanted to warm her up. I moved the white cloth at her head. 'Can I see her hair, please? I want to see her hair.'

They looked at each other. 'We had to shave some of it off for the post mortem,' one of them said.

I had really wanted to see her with her beautiful hair one more time. Later on I was told that they had shaved it all off. The irony didn't escape me. How many times had she told me that Rastafarians never cut their hair? Here she lay in death with all her lovely curls gone.

I could nearly hear her saying, 'Mum. They've made me into a "bald head". How could you let them?'

I bent to kiss her cold, still, porcelain cheek. That was all. What had it all been for? My own prediction of a few weeks earlier and all of Fiona's were fulfilled.

This, then, was death, the death of my child. No longer dancing, screaming, laughing, shocking and beautifully alive, but now, lying here so still. She wasn't a part of life any more. She was somewhere else where I was not privileged to be with her. I have not feared death since nor will I ever again.

As we left Doncaster, the news that the body in the car park had been identified was being released to the press. I was frantic to get back to my mother's flat to tell her before she heard it. We had just arrived when the four o'clock news came on the car radio: 'The body of the young woman found in a multi-storey car park in Doncaster has been identified as that of Fiona Ivison . . .'

I raced up to my Mum's flat, praying that she hadn't heard it. I unlocked her door and went in, followed by Graham. My mum was sitting in her chair by the fire.

I said a silent prayer, 'Oh God, help me to tell her.'

How do you tell an old woman of eighty-eight that her beloved grandchild has been murdered?

You should have had to tell her what you had done, Duffy, not me.

I knelt by her chair.

'What's wrong? Is there something wrong?' She was instantly alarmed.

'It's Fiona, Mum.' I stuttered out the dreadful words: 'She's dead. She's been murdered.'

My poor mum. All those years of struggle. Always living proudly and independently. Never knowingly hurting anyone. Always striving for her family and now, at the end of her years, when she should have been living peacefully, to have to endure this. She had loved Fiona as she loved all her grandchildren. When Fi was young they would spend hours playing together. Fi had often called in to see her granny on her own and would help her with shopping and other tasks. They were very close.

Brave as ever and with her inbuilt stoicism, my mum absorbed the dreadful news, got up, put on her coat and came back with me to Fenwick Road.

The next few weeks passed in a daze. We were all extremely shocked; our lives had taken on an unreal quality.

When my mother and I arrived back at Fenwick Road, after I had been to identify Fiona in Doncaster, we were met on the doorstep by a horde of newspaper reporters plus photographers and TV crews all anxious to get a picture of our grief. They were outside the house again the next morning. I had actually had some sleep that night with the aid of some prescribed drugs. When I went to draw back the curtains there they all were. I quickly pulled them to and realised they would have to stay closed for the rest of the day.

Graham arrived and suggested that the best thing to do about them was for the police to arrange a press conference in Doncaster that afternoon. The reporters could then be satisfied and, with any luck, would leave us alone, so I agreed.

The officer in charge of the investigation was

Detective Superintendent John Hope. That afternoon he accompanied me to the press conference. It was decided that I would say a short piece to the newsmen first, answer a few questions if I felt able, then leave and John would take over.

A sense of unreality overwhelmed me as I walked into the room set aside for the purpose. There was a table at which we took our places in front of the microphones. Whenever I see other parents doing the same thing, and there are so many of these occasions these days, I weep for them.

I tried to appeal to the better nature of the reporters. I was thinking of my mum, a thoroughly decent, respectable and proud woman. I couldn't bear the thought of her being hurt further, suffering at the hands of the press. I asked them to treat my family with some humanity. I told them that Fiona was a naive and innocent child, who had been lured into prostitution. I finished by appealing to anybody who had any information to come forward. I then spoke directly to Fiona's killer and asked him to give himself up.

'You are sick,' I said. 'You need help. Give yourself up before you do it again.'

There were a few questions, mainly about what Fiona was like, where she had gone to school and how were we coping.

Then someone asked, 'How did you feel, Mrs Ivison, when you were told what Fiona had been doing?'

I felt like saying, 'How the bloody hell do you think I felt?'

I managed to restrain myself and at that point John Hope rescued me and asked if I had had enough. I told him I had and Graham escorted me back up to John's office. I asked for a brandy and when one was produced gulped it down gratefully.

I cannot speak highly enough of the police who helped us at this time. Natalie basically held my house-hold together; she helped Rebecca and John so much. Despite his huge workload, John Hope always had time to answer our questions and kept us fully informed as events unfolded. Graham was the most involved with us: we can never repay his kindness.

If people only knew what these officers have to face: how they have to take mothers to identify dead chil-dren; how they have to see at first hand the raw grief of parents when they are told how dreadfully their child has died. How can they not be personally affected? We met with nothing but kindness from all of these officers. They showed us caring over and above the course of duty.

I wish I could have said the same for the press. The next day's papers had seized upon the story and did all they could to titillate their readers' appetites.

TWILIGHT WORLD OF FIONA.
SECRET SEX LIFE FIONA HID FROM HER MUM.

THE GIRL WHO ACTED OUT THE FANTASY OF PRETTY WOMAN.
ROOKIE HOOKER MURDERED.

There was nothing we could do about it. We just had to bear it. One of the papers even said that Fiona was known to the police, the implication being that she had a criminal record. The truth, of course, was that she was known to the police because of the times I had had to report her missing, during her under-age relationship with Elroy. Surprisingly, for one whose associates in life left a lot to be desired, she had no convictions whatsoever.

This treatment at the hands of the press added to our distress, but we were in no position to protest, so we just had to deal with it as best as we could at the time. We really began to find out who our true friends were, and they were many, more than enough to make up for this unkindness.

Thankfully, after the press conference the newshounds left my doorstep in search of other prey.

The next day Rebecca asked if she could see her sister. I was very uncertain what effect this might have on her, young as she was. Knowing how I felt myself, and my desperate need to see Fi and say goodbye to her properly, I didn't feel I had any right to deny Rebecca this opportunity, if it was what she wanted. I have to say, though, that I wasn't entirely sure whether it was the right thing to do or not. I was really concerned at what sort of long-lasting psychological effects this tragedy was going to have on both Rebecca and John. In the event I came to the conclusion that denying Rebecca this opportunity would cause more harm. I have found that the imagination can go into overdrive; in the end it is better to see or hear the truth and cope with it as a fact, than to try to deal with the endless horrors which the traumatised mind can so easily produce.

That afternoon Rebecca went with her father to Doncaster to say her last goodbye to her sister. She didn't say much when she got home but I knew that she was OK with the experience. She had asked to be left on her own with Fi and had half an hour with her. She had lain across her body and hugged her and told her how much she loved her. My 14 year old child's first encounter with death. I am reminded of the words from the bible:

> O death, where is thy sting?
> O grave, where is thy victory?

Although I was worried about it at the time I know now that this was the right decision.

The next time we all saw Fiona was in the chapel of rest before she was buried. Seeing someone who you have loved in life lying so still in death can bring home to you a certain reality. I personally felt a strong conviction that there had to be more to it than this. This really wasn't my daughter any more. I knew that her spirit was somewhere else. I felt very strongly that she still existed, for the time being out of reach. I could content myself with the thought that one day I too would be freed from these earthly ties.

A little glimmer of understanding started to grow within me; I began to realise that it was a triumphant Fiona now. Yes, I would weep and my grief and anger would be terrible, but the torment was mine and my family's, not Fi's any more. Yes, she had suffered, and I still can't bear to think of her last minutes, but that was over and done with for her. It was not happening now. At long last she was safe.

While we were dealing with these personal affairs the police investigation was in full swing. The morning following the identification, Zebbi was arrested. He was held at Doncaster Police Station and questioned. He was an obvious suspect. A neighbour had seen Fi get into his car on the Friday night, probably the last sighting of her in Sheffield. There was also our family testimony of her involvement with him in the preceding weeks.

I was told afterwards of the frustration the police endured in their dealings with this man. Residents of the street in Doncaster where Fi had stood to sell herself had noted a black man with dreadlocks waiting in the area for about three hours very late on Friday evening/Saturday morning. He was in a car similar to the one which Zebbi had apparently hired for the night. This is another trick of the pimp: a hire car rather than your own makes it more difficult for the police to catch up with you. Zebbi must have been very worried when Fiona failed to turn up. He had obviously waited a long time for her. I don't know whether he had any feelings for her then or whether he was more concerned not to be receiving the rest of that night's earnings. That part of me which has had the naivety knocked out of it believes it to be the latter.

He must also of course have realised by now that, in police jargon, he was 'in the frame'. The police were naturally very interested in what light he could throw on Fiona's murder. To their great chagrin, after admitting that he had taken Fiona out in his car that evening, he turned his face to the wall and insisted on his right to silence. I have since heard it said that this is a right which an innocent man almost never uses: he is too eager to prove that he is not guilty to remain silent when questioned.

Forensic tests were made on Zebbi's car and clothing. These proved nothing. Later we were to find out that he had not killed Fiona, so there would obviously not have been any blood or incriminating evidence. I hadn't really thought that Zebbi was the murderer. Why on earth would he have wanted to kill someone with such good earning potential? However, I felt then as I still feel now that he should have been charged with procuring a girl for the purpose of prostitution, and with living off immoral earnings. The police, to their great frustration, were not able to produce enough evidence to charge him. The Doncaster resident and two young women who had been working the street that same night and had also seen Fiona with a Rastafarian were unable to identify him.

That afternoon John Hope phoned to let us know that they had had to let Zebbi go without charge. At the same time he told us they had arrested another suspect. They had not charged this man with anything but they were certainly very interested in him.

That evening I came as close as I ever did to breaking down completely. It was the thought of Zebbi returning to his home just up the road from us. He might not have killed Fiona but to my mind he was every bit as responsible as the murderer. I looked at my shocked and grief-stricken family. So much pain. I thought of my fruitless battle to keep Fiona safe and now, even with her life so brutally ended, this man, who had preyed on her when she was fourteen, again totally unpunished and free to carry on his endless exploitation of other vulnerable girls.

Suddenly I had to get away. I said to Graham that I was going to crack up if I didn't escape somewhere, just for the night. I wanted to be knocked out. I didn't want to have to think about any of it. I wanted to stop my tortured mind for just a few hours and then I would face it again with renewed strength in the morning.

I walked out of the house that evening with nothing, no money, no nightclothes, just what I was wearing and a coat. My family were well looked after. My sister was with us by now, Natalie had come for the night and my mum was still there. I was enough in control not to want the children to be worried about me, so Graham told them I was just going to the police station to help with more enquiries.

It was around ten-thirty when we left. I asked Graham if he could take me to a hospital casualty department and ask them to sedate me for the night. I know he wanted to make sure that I was going to be all right. He rang the Hallamshire Hospital and explained the position. I'm not sure what their answer was but it quickly became plain that it wasn't going to be that easy to accommodate me. They promised to ring Graham back on his mobile phone. We cruised around the hospital area while we waited for a reply. Eventually the phone rang. There were no beds available. They advised Graham to ring my GP. This he did and once again we were told that my doctor would ring back.

We carried on cruising around Sheffield. By now it was nearly midnight. I was very aware that it must have been a long day for Graham and he must have been tired and longing to get back to his own home. I apologised to him and asked if it would be possible for me to spend the night in a cell in the police station. I thought a police doctor would be able to provide me with the necessary drugs to give me some oblivion. Although it sounds ludicrous now, at the time it seemed to be a good idea. Fortunately Graham didn't agree. At this point the phone in the car rang again. It was my own GP.

'Bring her round to my house,' was his kindly suggestion.

Dr Leigh lived not far from us, as it happened. It was well past midnight when we arrived. Realising that I was without money or possessions, Graham gave me a twenty pound note and saw me into the house.

It was humanity like this that pulled me through. Dr Leigh and his wife sat up with me and listened while I talked. It was the middle of the night and they must have been tired. They also had young children to get up for in the morning. We eventually went to bed. Dr Leigh had given me some tablets which certainly had the required effect. I slept peacefully, dreamlessly, a merciful rest for my poor battered mind. In the morning I was able to cope once again.

The following day was Christmas Eve. Graham called round and informed us that John Hope in Doncaster had some news for us. He was going to ring us in the afternoon to tell us what it was. We decided that it would be a good idea to take the call in my ex-husband's house where there were phone extensions and we'd all be able to hear what was being said at the same time.

At around 2 p.m. we all gathered near the phones.

John Hope's calm voice came over the line: 'We are charging a man with Fiona's murder. His name is Allan Duffy. He's a twenty-six-year-old white man. We arrested him on Thursday morning. We were fairly certain that we had the right man and this morning he has admitted his guilt.'

He then went on to tell us some more details of the arrest. Duffy had been particularly affected by my appearance on the TV. He had also asked John to tell us that he was sorry: he hadn't meant it to go that far.

I was glad that he'd been caught. At least we might now learn what had happened on that awful night. Nothing then could have made any of us feel any better, but I imagine we could have felt much worse if Fiona's murderer had eluded justice.

After this phone call Rebecca, John and I returned home. By now things were quieter and we were trying to get a little normality back into our routine. Some good friends of mine had done some shopping for us. I realised that I had barely eaten all week. I simply couldn't manage to swallow any food. I had such a tight knot in my stomach that every time I tried to eat I felt sick.

I knew that I had to make an effort for Rebecca and John and I was aware that the next day was Christmas

Day. The shopping my friends had bought included a small turkey. I was now in the minority in my family as a vegetarian and so I had to provide the meat eaters with the usual Christmas fare. My mother is famous in our family for making the most delicious home-made stuffing. She set to that afternoon to do her best for the kids. As she got on with cleaning out the bird she asked me if I had a needle and thread with which she could sew it up after she had stuffed it.

I'm ashamed to admit that I never ever do any sewing. I am so hopeless at it that I gave up trying years ago, so of course there was no needle in the house. I also realised that I hadn't bought enough small items for the kids' Christmas stockings. I decided to venture into town on my own and try to do some shopping.

I parked my car, without thinking, in a multi-storey car park in town. Then, as I walked down the stairs, I suddenly imagined Fi going so willingly to her death in a similar place in Doncaster. I screamed silently, gritted my teeth and went on.

All around me there was merriment and revelry. People were wearing party hats and singing drunkenly. There were crowds of happy faces doing their last-minute shopping.

I wanted to scream at them: 'Stop it. Do you know what has happened to me? Do you know what I have been given for Christmas?' But of course I didn't.

I managed to get some small bits and pieces that we

needed. Then I went into Atkinsons, a large department store where I knew I'd be able to buy the needle and cotton. For some reason, although I knew the store well, I couldn't find the haberdashery counter. I became really upset, as if I was about to burst into tears at my stupidity. I longed to be back in the cocooned safety of my own home, where nobody expected me to know what I was doing, where everyone knew it would be a long time before any of us felt even remotely like a normal person going about their daily activity.

I decided I'd have to ask an assistant for help. I approached the nearest one and said, 'Please can you help me? You see my daughter has just been murdered and I need to buy a needle and thread so my mother can sew up the turkey. I can't seem to find what I want. Please will you help me?' The young shop assistant didn't turn a hair. 'Oh dear,' she said, and scurried off to fetch what I needed.

Occasionally I feel embarrassed at how I behaved in those early days. I had to talk and talk about it to anybody who would listen. This is a healthy reaction and part of the healing process, but it is perhaps unfair to burden your friends with such tremendous sorrow.

I can only say to those who had to put up with my rantings: I am sorry if it was hard for you, but you helped me tremendously at the time and, by taking just a little of my grief, you made it easier for me. There was no escape from it at all for me. Every waking moment I went over and over it in my mind. The only release was sleep. How I loved to sleep. I would collapse, exhausted, and pray that I wouldn't wake up in the night. When I did, the horror of it all gripped me again as if it had only just happened. I would wake up crying and searching for Fiona.

'Where is she?' I would scream, silently. 'I can't find her. Oh God. Help me.'

Nevertheless life went on and Christmas Day dawned on my family the same as it did for everyone else. I lit the fire and we opened our presents. We were all thinking of Fi and missing her terribly. I kept thinking that she had no presents.

I couldn't bear the thought of how this man who had killed her must have hated her. She didn't deserve to die like that. I know she wouldn't have wanted to hurt him. She just wasn't like that.

Then the phone rang. It was John Hope ringing to see how we were. It suddenly came to me what I wanted to do.

'John,' I said. 'Can you tell me how to get to the car park in Doncaster where Fiona died? I want to take her some flowers. That's all I can do for her now. I just want to give her something for Christmas.'

He understood. 'I'll come right over and take you there.'

This was typical of the kindness we had received all the time from the police. John had his own family to go to on Christmas Day, yet he spared the time for us. It says a lot for these officers' wives and families, who have to be very supportive in these circumstances.

It wasn't long before John picked us up in his car and drove us to Doncaster. Rebecca and John had decided to come too. We drove through a deserted Doncaster. John showed us the street where Fi had stood and then he took us on her last journey to the car park. The stairwell where she had died was boarded up. The spot was right on the top of the car park. Closer to heaven. It was cold and windy up there. We laid all our flowers at the entrance and stood in the bitter December air and hugged each other.

After this journey with John we all felt better. I'm sure Fi knew that we had thought of her. Although it might seem as if I was fooling myself that I could still give her presents, in the circumstances it seemed a harmless piece of self-deception.

Only two people know exactly how Fiona died, and only one of them is able to give an account of what actually happened.

It can be very difficult to get information about the murder of a family member. The reason, I am told, is that nothing must be done which might jeopardise a fair trial. We cannot hand to the defence counsel any indication that information has been released which might result in adverse publicity for the defendant. On these grounds alone, a trial could possibly be abandoned, allowing a guilty man to evade justice on a mere technicality.

I recently heard a psychiatrist talking of the need for those bereaved by murder to be given full information as soon as possible, so that they can face what actually happened and then start to deal with it. He obviously hadn't had to deal with our criminal justice system. Having said this, I do know that in Fiona's case, I was given as much information as possible, by both the police and the prosecution team.

Michael Murphy, the prosecuting QC, and his junior counsel, Gary Burrell, set aside time for us to ask questions after each pre-trial hearing. In the end we were spared the ordeal of a full trial as Allan Duffy pleaded guilty to murder. This does not happen very often, apparently, as the mandatory sentence for murder is life, and most killers will at least try to get away with the lesser charge of manslaughter.

The following account of what happened on that night is taken from the transcript prepared by prosecuting counsel for the trial judge, and from various newspaper reports. After Duffy was sentenced, I asked for and was freely given the transcript.

Allan Paul Duffy was born on 27 January 1967. He was twenty-six when he killed my daughter.

Duffy had three children of his own, a fact which leaves me wondering how he could have harmed my child, because in truth Fiona was little more than a child. He must have known when he walked with her on that last journey that this was only a youngster he had picked up.

He had been married to Karen Duffy, the mother of two of his children. They were divorced in 1989. Duffy tried, and failed, to get custody of his children. He had then set up home in Doncaster with his girlfriend, and they had a baby girl. At the time of Fiona's murder, Duffy's own child was six months old.

That particular evening, Duffy had money in his

pocket. He and his girlfriend were about to move from their bedsit in Balby Road to a semi-detached house in the outskirts of Doncaster. They had applied for and been given a community care grant to help them furnish their new home. The DSS had sent two cheques to a total value of £425, which were cashed straight away. Duffy was unemployed and also received income support of £77 a week.

I find it particularly ironic that the welfare state, which I have always defended to the hilt, should have provided this man with the money to murder my daughter. If we had a fairer society it would not be necessary to subsidise people in this way. While I accept that there are genuinely needy people, it does cross my mind that when large sums of money are given for a specific purpose, there should be some way of checking that this is what the cash is actually used for. It is this sort of abuse of the system which turns moderate people against the welfare state.

That evening, after hugging her granny at our home, Fiona had left Sheffield with Zebbi at about seven-thirty. At around nine, two young women from Leeds arrived in the red light area of Doncaster, intending to work the street that night. They noticed Fiona sitting in the passenger seat of a white motor car in Vaughn Avenue with a black male Rastafarian in the driver's seat. There is no doubt in my mind that this was Zebbi. They then saw her leave the car and stand on a corner near by.

In my mind's eye I can see Fi as she stood there. She would have been pretending that she was used to doing this sort of thing. We know from the pathologist's report that she had been smoking marijuana. I personally think and, indeed, hope that she was in 'dreamland'. She must have been cold. She was wearing only the Lycra top which Zebbi had bought her and a mini skirt with tights or leggings under a short black jacket. Being only slight, she felt the cold. She must also have felt very lonely. She clearly didn't know the other girls and I am sure that if they had spoken to her they would have thought she was stuck up; either that or really weird, if she attempted to act out the role in which Zebbi had cast her.

At about ten, Duffy arrived in the area. Duffy was no stranger to using the services of prostitutes. He approached one of the young women from Leeds and asked her for 'business'. She suggested they go to an alleyway, but he walked away from her, saying he would think about it.

A short while later he approached the other girl from Leeds and asked her for 'business'. She accepted and walked with him to an alleyway close to Glyn Avenue. He chatted to her as they walked, telling her that he had an unfurnished house in Thorne and that they had just had the carpets fitted. They reached the alleyway and Duffy attempted intercourse, but was unable to complete the act. When the girl indicated to him that 'time was money', he produced a wad of £50 notes (the social security money), bragging that money was no problem. They continued for a short while but Duffy was still unable to ejaculate. At this point he indicated that he would try with her friend. She pointed out that her companion was with a client but wouldn't be long. She left him standing on the corner of Vaughn Avenue.

By now it was about ten-thirty. This young woman left the area with another client for fifteen minutes. On her return she saw Duffy and Fiona together, walking from Vaughn Avenue into Christchurch Road and then into Park Road towards the town centre. By now it was about 10.50 p.m. This was the last time Fiona was seen alive.

The walk from the red light area to the Northern Bus Station car park would have taken approximately twenty minutes. I wonder what they talked about as they made Fi's last journey. Maybe they made casual conversation. I wonder if she told him about me and about her brother and sister. I wonder if he talked about his own little ones. What must he have thought of her? He said afterwards that he couldn't make her out. One minute she was talking in this posh voice, and the next she was trying to speak like a Jamaican. Oh, Fiona, I can't believe even now that you did it.

Duffy, a man with obvious sexual problems, must have been feeling anxious at his inability to perform earlier on. I suppose he wasn't wise enough to realise that what he needed was counselling and therapy, not a drugged up, bullied teenager, who really would have no idea what to do to help him.

They reached the car park at about 11.10 p.m. He then took her right up to the top floor. I have been to the spot where she died a few times since. It is cold and lonely.

Not long left to live now, Fiona. Don't be frightened, my child.

Fifteen minutes into the sex act and Duffy was experiencing problems again. Fiona must have been anxious to get back to Zebbi and aware that she had a long walk back she started to tell him that he had had long enough.

At that point Duffy's rage and frustration boiled over. Fiona attempted to sit up and he pushed her back down roughly to the ground. Her head hit the floor and she started to scream. Duffy put his hand over her mouth and told her to stop screaming. In the circumstances, a more experienced woman might just have survived. But Fi was not such a person.

Where were you, Zebbi, pimp? I thought it was your role to protect her. Did you not even warn Fiona of the dangers of moving out of the area? Sure, you provided the dope to enable her to earn for you, but was that where your responsibility ended? Well, listen now to how she died. See it in your mind and imagine her horror.

My poor child must have been so frightened. When Duffy removed his hand, she started to scream again, signing her own death warrant. He grabbed her head by the hair at both sides and repeatedly banged it down on to the concrete of the car-park floor. He then placed his hand across her throat and strangled her, leaning on her with the full weight of his body. She died from the injuries to her head and neck.

The car park was quiet once again, apart from the angels singing.

I now began the sad task of sorting out Fiona's belongings. I sat in her room and held each of her things to me. A faint smell of her perfume on some clothing would have me hugging the item to myself and rocking in my grief. Then I came across a sheet of foolscap paper. The whole of Psalm 37 was written out on it in Fiona's neat script. 'Fret not because of evil men . . .' It was almost as if she had left it for me.

Psalm 37

1 Fret not because of evil men
    or be envious of those who do wrong;
2 for like the grass they will soon wither,
    like green plants they will soon die away.
3 Trust in the LORD and do good;
    dwell in the land and enjoy safe pasture.
4 Delight yourself in the LORD
    and he will give you the desires of your heart.
5 Commit your way to the LORD;
    trust in him and he will do this:
6 He will make your righteousness shine like the dawn,
    the justice of your cause like the noonday sun.
7 Be still before the LORD and wait patiently for him;
    do not fret when men succeed in their ways,
    when they carry out their wicked schemes.
8 Refrain from anger and turn from wrath;
    do not fret – it leads only to evil.
9 For evil men will be cut off,
    but those who hope in the LORD will inherit the land.
10 A little while, and the wicked will be no more;
    though you look for them, they will not be found.
11 But the meek will inherit the land
    and enjoy great peace.
12 The wicked plot against the righteous
    and gnash their teeth at them;
13 but the LORD laughs at the wicked,
    for he knows their day is coming.
14 The wicked draw the sword and bend the bow
    to bring down the poor and needy,
    to slay those whose ways are upright.
15 But their swords will pierce their own hearts,
    and their bows will be broken.

In the drawer beside it there was a £20 note. There was no other money. I suddenly remembered as if it was yesterday the bet I had made with Fi when she was fifteen. We had been talking about prostitution. She had promised me that she would never become a prostitute and we had had a light-hearted bet about it. If she continued to mix in the company she was keeping and had not become a prostitute by the time she was twenty-one, I would give her £20; if, on the other hand, she had allowed herself to be drawn into the trade, she would give me £20.

It may have been coincidence that this was the only money that she left. It's also possible that Fi, convinced her death was not far off and realising she had lost the bet, left the money for me deliberately, almost as if she was saying, 'You were right, Mum, and I'm sorry.'

A few days after Christmas a letter with a Humberside postmark arrived for me. It was from Elroy in the Wolds Prison. He sent me a letter he had received from Fiona just before she died. He also asked me to come and see him. He sounded wretched and unhappy.

Fi had written him a beautiful letter. She apologised for not visiting him. She told him she still loved him and spoke again of their dream of going to live in Ethiopia.

The longer I stay in this terrible place, the more I

realise that evil forces always hold me back from what I try to do.

Then she mentions her belief that she had lived before:

I have also discovered who I have been and it helps me to understand what I am now. Can you understand this? Is a person's identity their body and their outwardly appearance or is it what's inside, their soul? You see I have been in a situation where some bad things have happened to me and I have been able to match these events exactly to what happened in Egypt. After my oppressors had let me go, they changed their minds and came for me but I am protected. Elroy, I know this probably sounds really nutty, but it is not something that I have been taught by something outside. It is something inside which can be discovered when you leave behind things created by this society to corrupt a person's mind.

She ends her letter on yet another prophetic note:

I hope you're allright, Elroy. It might be a long time but it won't be forever and one day we'll be free and I don't just mean out of there, I mean really free. Elroy, write to me soon. I love getting your letters.

She ends the letter: 'JAH LOVE, QUEEN OMEGA.'

I am not clear about the Queen Omega reference. I only know that Omega is the last letter of the Greek alphabet. Perhaps this is yet another indication of Fiona's premonitions that her own ending was very near.

Rebecca, John and I decided that Fi would have wanted us to visit Elroy.

A few days later we set out in the car for the Wolds. This is a comparatively modern men's prison, run by the security firm, Group 4.

On arrival we found the reception area. I had never been in a prison before and hadn't a clue what we were supposed to do. The room was full of women and their children. All the women seemed to be chain smoking and the air was thick with stale smoke. We gave our names in to the officer at the desk, who allocated us a number and told us to wait our turn. It was a long wait. Eventually our number was called. We had to go through security searches and were given identity tags and then proceeded through the locked gates into the prison itself.

The visiting room was a large hall filled with tables, each with four chairs and a number. At the top of the room the prison officers sat at a table. Behind them was a door through which the prisoners entered the room and which was unlocked and locked each time someone came in.

We were told to go to table number 6 and wait. We had to sit there for about ten minutes. Everywhere I looked round the room the women were trying to touch their men with love. The children ran around, for the most part ignored by their parents, apart from the odd shouted rebuke when one of them misbehaved a bit too obviously. The prison officers patrolled up and down between the tables.

Eventually the door from the prison was unlocked and Elroy appeared. He came straight over to us and I took his hand. I couldn't hate him now: he had loved Fiona and she had loved him. I know that any harm he may have done to her was unintentional. I had felt that their relationship was abusive when she was so young; I still think she was harmed by what she was exposed to at a time and an age when she was very vulnerable. But I also know that Elroy and I were vastly different people with chasms between us in terms of culture. What to me was wrong, to Elroy was acceptable. What to me was a drug, to Elroy was a 'holy herb'.

We sat down at the table.

'Irene, tell me what happened,' he said. 'What the papers have been saying about Fiona. It can't be true.'

'Yes, it is,' I told him. I saw two big tears trickle down his face.

I then told him about Zebbi and how I had not known what was going on until after Fiona was murdered.

Elroy's face was so sad. 'It's all my fault,' he said. 'She hated me stealing. If I hadn't been in prison, then none of this would have happened. Many a time when she was with me, men would come up to me, big men from London, and they would ask me to let them take Fiona to London. They said she would earn big money there as a prostitute, but I always protected her from them. I even hit one of them once.'

'I know, Elroy,' I said. 'Fiona loved you. She told me shortly before she died that she would always love you.'

His face changed. 'She knew that she was going to die,' he told me. 'She was always saying she would die when she was young. I wonder how she knew.'

Another of Fi's companions to whom she had entrusted her knowledge of her destiny.

Then I remembered the engagement ring Elroy had given Fiona. Shortly after she died I had gone to see Sandra, her best friend from the square. Sandra had promised to find Yvonne, who had so cruelly ripped the ring from Fi's finger, and try to get it back. I asked Elroy what he would like me to do with the ring.

His face darkened with anger. 'Oh yes,' he said, 'people can get it back for her now, now that she's dead. But no one cared enough to get it back for her when she was alive.'

I hadn't thought of it in that way. 'I just thought that you might have liked it to be buried with her, Elroy,' I said.

His expression softened. 'Yes, you do that,' he said.

Then I told him what we had arranged for Fiona's funeral. I also told him that her hair had been shaved off.

'They would be trying to stop her spirit from going to God,' he muttered.

Our time was drawing to a close and all round us the room was emptying. We walked with Elroy back to the door leading to the cells. Then we said goodbye. He shook hands with John and pressed knuckle to knuckle with Rebecca. I looked at him and then he put his arms around me and we hugged each other. We must have looked a strange sight, the dreadlocked Rastafarian embracing the middle-aged woman. We had both loved my daughter in our different ways and for that moment and for all time we are united in our grief.

I have not seen Elroy since that meeting, nor am I likely to. I hope that for Fiona's sake he will get his life together and that, when he comes out of prison, with his debt to society paid, he will be able to find some peace and harmony in his life as he lives out his span. I know that she will be looking out for him.

I shall never be able to harbour any fond feelings for the other Rastafarian who featured in Fiona's life. I was faced daily with the prospect of seeing his car go up and down our road. In my imagination I vented my fury on that car. I wanted to paint 'PIMP' on it in large black letters, and then I wanted to take a brick and smash it to bits. I really felt that given the chance I might do something extreme to Zebbi himself, not just his car. How I wanted to make him suffer. Not physically, I'm sure he's used to that, but mentally. I thought that if he had to endure only a small fraction of the torture he'd subjected me to, then he might, conceivably, realise what he had done. I didn't want revenge. I just wanted him to be sorry. I wanted him to tell me that he would stop exploiting these young women for his own gain, and that never again would he take a girl like Fiona to her death.

In the circumstances we had to move away from Fenwick Road. None of us could have coped with seeing Zebbi every day. I was very fortunate in that my employers, the Sheffield Children's Hospital, were extremely helpful and considerate. Almost immediately they offered us a small flat near the hospital, which we gratefully accepted.

One evening, however, before we moved, I did have an encounter with Zebbi. I was pulling into our house when he drove up in his car. He had to stop to allow me to reverse into the drive. When I realised it was him, I shook my fists at him, parked the car and walked up the road to where he was getting out of his car. He sat on the wall outside his house as I shouted at him.

'I want you to listen to what I have to say to you. As far as I am concerned you are as responsible for

Fiona's death as the man who killed her. We all know you took her to Doncaster. We all know you made her stand on the streets and sell herself. You may have escaped justice in this world, but one day you will have to face your maker, and I wouldn't be in your shoes then.'

At this point he interjected, 'I'm not a pimp. I'm a musician.'

This made me explode again. 'We *know* that you are a pimp. I tell you now, Simpson, that I put a mother's curse on you. You will walk this earth cursed for what you did to Fiona. You are cursed until you are sorry. Take those other girls off the streets. You work for *them* for a change. I curse you, Simpson. Until the end of my days, I will walk past this house and I will curse you until you are sorry. *You* are Babylon.'

He started to chant in some language I didn't recognise. Maybe he was trying to ward off my curses.

'I curse you. I curse you. I curse you.' I screamed it at him again and again.

Then I had had enough of it. It was futile anyway. I left him to do whatever he would with his conscience. I could make no difference to a man like him.

On a bright morning in the middle of January we buried our child. She was wearing a dress of Sandra's, one Fiona had always admired when Sandra wore it on their evenings out together. Sandra wanted Fiona to have it, her last gift to her friend. I had put Elroy's ring back on her finger. Her head was swathed in a turban, African style, and a coloured scarf covered the strangulation marks on her slender neck. Robert and Fringe, her childhood toys, lay beside her in her coffin along with some treasured photos.

We and our friends said our goodbyes to her in the Catholic Church of Our Lady and St Thomas. My friends and the parish priest organised the service. They read from Martin Luther King, Anne Frank and other peace-loving idealists. We sang songs from Greenham Common and heard Whitney Houston belt out a favourite for the kids.

I knew that really I should have asked people to make donations to charity instead of giving flowers, but this time I wanted Fi to have loads of flowers as she left us. I kept thinking about her lying all night on her own in that cold, lonely car park and I wanted to make it up to her somehow. So she had flowers heaped high on her coffin, a beautiful, colourful display.

The sun shone brightly all that January morning and it didn't stop shining until we had buried Fi in the ground in the cemetery in Abbey Lane.

That night I dreamed of Zebbi. For some reason I was driving Rebecca and John to a party in Broomhall, when suddenly a car drew up alongside us, forcing us to slow down. When I looked across I saw that it was Zebbi driving this other car. But it was a very strange Zebbi:

his face was anguished with a terrible sorrow, he had cut his long dreadlocks and his hair had turned grey. He didn't say anything. He just looked at me. Then suddenly his face changed, but only slightly, and I realised that it had become the face of his mother. The sadness in that face was hard to look upon. I woke up once again crying.

The grief and anguish following the murder of someone you have loved are hard to describe. There is no magic wand to make it better. You have to accept that for a long, long time you are not going to feel normal. It is no good pretending that you are the same as you were before. In a small moment your life has been changed, utterly, and you know it will never be the same again.

There are, however, some comforts, and even though at the time of writing less than two years have passed since Fiona died, I am able to feel positive about my life and the future.

For a long time, I experienced what I can only call appalling 'visions' of the scene in the car park as Duffy murdered Fiona. One night I had gone to bed and was drifting off to sleep when suddenly I was again there with her in the car park. This time it was the worst I had yet experienced. I could actually feel her heart-stopping fear. My own heart raced and I was terrified. I saw her eyes staring out of her head as she died. It was as if I was there in her body as he killed her.

I screamed out in terror, 'I can't stand this any more. I am mad. I am insane.'

And then something wonderful happened. In an instant my fear completely evaporated and I was bathed in the most beautiful, loving, warm light. I felt as if I was in the presence of a power so good and wonderful that no harm or suffering could touch me. In that light I was loved and safe. I stayed in it all that night.

I often think of this experience and I have been tremendously helped by it. The scientists would say, I am sure, that it was the reaction of the traumatised brain to circumstances which could destroy a person's sanity. I feel in my heart that it is not so. It was the same light I saw the night my father-in-law died. The same light, I imagine, that people who have had 'near death' experiences have so often described. To me it was an intensely spiritual experience. Ever since I have been convinced that Fiona is in that beautiful light and I am happy for her. I can let her go because I know that she is safe.

Sometimes now I close my eyes and I can see her again. I can see her oh so clearly.

There's Fiona and Dawn, 'little' Pete, James and Maureen. All our murdered children. Their bodies are whole, no terrible injuries. They look so happy.

My friends, we will be with them again. We will fill our lives as best we can with loving and caring for others. We will not hold bitterness in our hearts against those who have so hurt us, for in the great eternal scheme they will one day have to face what they have done. We should only feel great sorrow for them. Not one of us with our terrible load of sorrow would swap places with them.

Time will pass and our wounds will heal. Not only that, it will bring us closer to the time when we too will be in that wonderful light with our dear children. It will be our time then, and nothing will ever take them away from us again.

Epilogue

It is over two years now since Fiona was murdered. Not a day goes by when she is not in my thoughts. I love her now as when she was alive. She is still my child. If I live to be a hundred years old, I will never forget her and what happened to us. But I do not intend to live out my life miserably, in anger, grief and despair. My experiences over the last years have changed me tremendously and I feel very strong. I do not wish to be pitied or seen as a tragic figure, because that is not what I am. I carry with me a great burden of sadness but I am learning to live with it because I know it will never leave me. The sorrow has to be put in its place and controlled, so that it doesn't take over.

In the same way all the negative aspects of life in our society today have somehow to be countered. I believe that the Zebbis and Duffys of this world have never learned to love. This is an appalling lack in their lives, for which they must be pitied. In the short term of course we have to protect society from such people, but in the longer term we do need to look at the conditions which create people with such an incredible lack of compassion and control.

What on earth did I ever do to you, Zebbi, that you could use my daughter in that way? You, Duffy, never even knew Fiona or my family, yet after a short meeting you saw fit to end her life. I hope you two can reflect upon your actions. Ask yourself: was it fair? Even if life had given you great hardship and sorrow, was your only answer to deal the same hand to someone else?

My life has changed so much since that terrible night. It has a new sharpness and appreciation. Things which were once important to me are now meaningless. I have an entirely new perspective on everything. I no longer feel normal, whatever that is.

For quite a while after Fiona died I did try to carry on as I had before. After two months' absence, I returned to work. I used to drive myself there crying all the way. When I arrived I would frantically repair my face and try to look as if I was coping. I don't think I really fooled anyone. I would sit in my office and try to concentrate on work but find myself staring out of the window for hours on end. Everybody, including the children at Oakes Park School, was so kind to me. On one occasion a little boy with a severe progressive disability came up to me and piped, 'Mrs Ivison, me mam says I have to say something to you.'

This was said in front of some visitors I was showing

around the department. With bated breath I asked him what it was.

'Me mam says I've to give you a big hug.'

How I loved him and his mum for that.

If there was gossip about Fiona's prostitution activity, it never reached me once. People were very considerate. Nevertheless I started to flounder.

The effects of murder go very deep. My feelings fluctuated between heart-wrenching grief, terrible anger, sickening fear and anxiety for my other two children and a black depression. Even after my wonderful experience of the light I continued to suffer dreadfully from the appalling visions of Fiona's death in the car park. I didn't know what to do to stop these experiences until I was fortunate enough to encounter John Hattersley. I met John on a management course I was doing from the Children's Hospital. He was acting as my mentor on this course and he also happened to be a psychologist. He gave me a lot of his time and a lot of very good advice. He taught me that I could and must take control of my mind in these instances. It was John who gave me the shove out of self-pity and apathy and the inspiration to regain control of my life. As if that wasn't enough, he pushed me to try to make something positive come out of this tragedy. I also had some very good counselling from Cruse.

The other problem that all my family suffered from was appalling anxiety. We were all terribly afraid that some other dreadful event was going to happen to one of us. We had moved away from Fenwick Road into some hospital accommodation shortly after the murder. We were given a one-bedroomed flat at first and quite soon moved to another with two bedrooms. This meant that Rebecca and John could each have a bedroom and I slept in the lounge. But it wasn't long before Rebecca started to join me at night in the lounge. Soon, after an appalling nightmare in which he saw his sister dying in the car park, John pulled his mattress into the lounge as well and we all slept together. This cosy arrangement lasted for most of that first year until we moved into our present house.

I used to moan about one or other of the children joining us in bed when they were very young, and people said, 'Cheer up. They won't be doing it when they're teenagers.' I remembered it then and thought how strange life was. It made the three of us very close.

One evening I went with John to pick Rebecca up. She was a few minutes late and as we sat waiting John said to me, 'You know, Mum, if anything has happened to Rebecca I'm going to kill myself.'

'Don't worry, John,' I said. 'We'll do it together.'

We were discussing the best way to do this and had decided on fixing a hose on to the exhaust pipe when Rebecca turned up.

Rebecca, too, became extremely anxious and disturbed. She would often turn to me and say, 'Mum, you're not going to die, are you?' I had to reassure her constantly that nothing was going to happen to me.

I was churned up and in such turmoil. My emotions were always just on the surface. I could cry and cry and cry. I spent whole days helplessly crying, especially when I was on my own. Rebecca was also seriously affected. She never managed to resume her schooling. She had actually just started her GCSEs, but it soon became apparent that she was not going to be able to cope with school. She had been badly damaged by the struggle we had had to help Fiona over the years preceding her murder.

At some point along the way I understood that we could not just carry on as if nothing had happened. I came to the conclusion that Rebecca's mental health was more important than her exams. I also realised that the only solution was for me to give up my job and stay at home and look after them both. This action in conjunction with some very good psychiatric help from the Northern General Hospital (the same unit which had not proved useful for Fiona) paid dividends. Slowly we all started to improve.

The other emotion which had to be dealt with was anger. I was so angry I sometimes didn't know what to do with myself. I used to take the car out into Derbyshire, drive into some remote area and scream. I would hear this terrible demented screaming like a madwoman or someone possessed and realise that it was me. Strangely enough this sort of weird behaviour is very beneficial. The screaming released my tension and anger and I would feel much more peaceful afterwards. As time went by I needed to do this less and less. I also came to understand that if I could direct and channel this anger, something good might arise from our experience.

It was at this stage that I met Diana Lamplugh, the mother of Suzy, who went missing ten years ago and is presumed murdered. Along with a group of other people we have set up an active campaigning organisation called Victim's Voice. We strive for a fairer and more just society and aim to be advocates for victims of serious crime in instances where justice does not seem to have been done.

I also started to take a very serious look at how children and young women are being exploited in prostitution today. The more I dug into the subject the more appalled I became at how easy it is for pimps to operate. Many factors contribute to this situation. The most striking is the attitude of the media which places all the blame on the girls themselves, depicting them as 'slags' and 'tarts', or some sort of different species or underclass. At the same time they pay scant attention to the scandal of the pimps who initially lure the youngsters into prostitution and then control them so they never escape. As I investigated I met many families very similar to mine whose youngsters had been sucked into this trade. Far from the usual picture drawn by the media, these families were decent, caring people who had simply been unable to compete against the pimps' influence and had found themselves, as I had when Fiona went off with Zebbi for the two nights when she was fourteen, powerless to stop the exploitation. None had been assisted by the interventions of the law or social services. It was for this reason that I started to campaign, in a small way, to raise public awareness about the plight of the families whose daughters have been abused and exploited in prostitution. It makes a little bit of sense out of my experience if what happened to me can be used to prevent the same thing happening to other innocent girls like Fiona.

I believe I have developed spiritually because of my experiences. More than I ever did before, I know that to love and care for people is a great strength. It is the only answer to the problems in today's society. At the same time we have to speak out against what is wrong. We can no longer be silent about injustices and endure the consequences of a greedy, hypocritical and corrupt society. Each of us in our own way can influence others by our actions. It is the only answer. Sometimes we may feel that justice has not been done. Certainly in my own case I feel that Zebbi's pimping should have been stopped. Maybe this will happen one day, maybe not. It is something I have to deal with; indeed it has been one of the hardest facts for me to cope with.

One of the people who helped me with this is Matthew Mark, who wrote to me out of the blue after reading about Fiona's murder in the national newspapers. Matthew's letters were full of hope and very positive. He explained to me the sense and natural justice of the theories of reincarnation or Karma. There is nothing more certain than the fact that we all live and that in the end our bodies will all perish. We can regard our span on this earth as a learning period for our spiritual entity. We may use our time here positively and grow and progress so that when our earthly hours are finished we can move into that state of spiritual peace which I would like to believe is like my wonderful light visions.

Alternatively we may not learn anything while we are here. We may be cruel and abuse others. We may live unwisely. Karma dictates that if we do this then we will need to live again in another life. We will be given the chance to learn again and to progress forwards spiritually. It may be that we will have to suffer in order to progress.

It is a system of natural justice way beyond the control of mankind and it ensures that in the end the values of love, truth and honesty are triumphant. It makes a lot more sense than just one chance in life with either Heaven or Hell at the end of it. I am still basically the sort of person who flounders in relation to all this, but I must say that the theory of Karma or natural justice has a lot of appeal for me.

And so life goes on for us all. I am changed and a lot of the time I feel apart from other people because of my experiences. But I have a new set of friends now, belonging to an organisation called SAMM (Support after Murder and Manslaughter). We have all been bereaved as a result of murder or manslaughter. We try to help each other through our pain and anger and find comradeship through our shared grief. We try to make some sense out of our tragedies and to raise some awareness about the plight of the victim in our circumstances. I have been greatly helped by SAMM and indeed by all the people who reached out to us both in a professional capacity and as friends.

I end on a happy note. Almost two years after Fiona died, Rebecca had a baby daughter, my granddaughter. She is God's gift to us. In our eyes a more beautiful, perfect child has never existed. The baby, John, Rebecca and I all live together happily and safely. They are in regular contact with their father and his wife who supports and cares for them too. We have much to look forward to. We remember our other daughter and sister with love. We remember her as she was, a bright, shining child.

This book was written for her. For Fiona with love.

Useful Addresses

CROP
P.O. Box 336,
Sheffield, S7 2YL
A campaigning group aiming to raise public awareness concerning the role of the pimp in prostitution.

SAMM
Cranmer House,
39 Brixton Road,
London SW9 6DZ
A self help group which supports those bereaved by murder or manslaughter.

VICTIMS VOICE
P.O. Box 7277,
London E11 3UB
A campaigning group working to promote justice for victims of serious crime.

THE SUZY LAMPLUGH TRUST
14 East Sheen Avenue,
London SW14 8AS
The national charity for personal safety.